Evil After Postmodernism

Evil After Postmodernism brings together a collection of six essays by a group of distinguished scholars which address our understanding of evil in the light of postmodern thought. The essays in this volume ask what might be lost without the concept of evil and what dangers might be incurred by continuing to use it. The essays are organized around three themes – Histories of Evil, Narratives of Evil, and Ethics of Evil. In each section the first essay illustrates certain theoretical difficulties faced by thinking about evil in the postmodern age, while the second offers a constructive response to these difficulties.

- Evil Inside and Outside History: The Post-Holocaust vs. the Postmodern
- On Contingency and Culpability: Is the Postmodern Post-Tragic?
- Narrating Evil. Great Faults and "Splendidly Wicked People"
- The Plot of Suffering: AIDS and Evil
- The Reflexivity of Evil: Modernity and Moral Transgression in the War in Bosnia
- Others and Aliens: Between Good and Evil

Jennifer L. Geddes' introduction opens this stimulating and lucid investigation into the meaning of evil following the enormous cultural and social changes of the postmodern age.

Jennifer L. Geddes is Research Assistant Professor in Religious Studies at the University of Virginia, Editor of *The Hedgehog Review,* and Co-Program Director and Permanent Fellow at the Institute for Advanced Studies in Culture, Virginia.

Evil After Postmodernism

Histories, Narratives, and Ethics

Edited by **Jennifer L. Geddes**

London and New York

First published 2001
by Routledge
11 Fetter Lane, London EC4P 4EE

Simultaneously published in the USA and Canada
by Routledge
29 West 35th Street, New York, NY 10001

Routledge is an imprint of the Taylor & Francis Group

Typeset in Times by Exe Valley Dataset Ltd, Exeter
Printed and bound in Great Britain by
TJ International Ltd, Padstow, Cornwall

British Library Cataloguing in Publication Data
A catalogue record for this book is available
from the British Library

Library of Congress Cataloging in Publication Data
A catalogue record for this book has been requested

ISBN 0–415–22815–8 (hbk)
ISBN 0–415–22816–6 (pbk)

Contents

List of Contributors

Larry D. Bouchard, Associate Professor of Religion and Literature at the University of Virginia, has taught and written extensively on the topics of evil, suffering, tragedy, negativity, and theodicy. He is the author of numerous articles, chapters, and books, including *Tragic Method and Tragic Theology: Evil in Contemporary Drama and Religious Thought* and "Holding Fragments: Medicine and Practical Theodicy" in *Theodicy and Medicine*, edited by Margaret Mohrmann and Mark Hanson.

Thomas Cushman is Associate Professor of Sociology and Whitehead Professor of Critical Thought at Wellesley College. He has published numerous papers and books on Soviet society and the Balkans and has co-edited, with Stjepan G. Meštrović, *This Time We Knew: Western Responses to Genocide in Bosnia*. Professor Cushman is the general editor for the series "Post-Communist Societies and Cultures" and the editor of *Human Rights Review*.

Jennifer L. Geddes is Research Assistant Professor of Religious Studies at the University of Virginia, Permanent Fellow and Co-Program Director of the Institute for Advanced Studies in Culture, and the Editor of *The Hedgehog Review: Critical Reflections on Contemporary Culture*. She is currently writing a book that focuses on the works of Franz Kafka and the connections between interpretive practices and ethical decisions, particularly in relation to power and violence.

Richard Kearney is Professor of Philosophy at University College Dublin and Visiting European Professor at Boston College. The author of thirteen books, including *Postnationalist Ireland, Poetics of Modernity*, and *Modern Movements in European Philosophy*, Professor Kearney has also edited eleven volumes, including *Continental Philosophy in the Twentieth Century, Paul Ricoeur: Hermeneutics of Action*, and *Across the Frontiers: Ireland in the 1990s*. He has published interviews with many of the leading contemporary thinkers, including Kristeva, Ricoeur, Steiner, Derrida, Levinas, Gadamer, and Lyotard.

Berel Lang is Professor of Humanities at Trinity College in Hartford, Connecticut. His work has spanned a wide range of topics, including

Marxism and art, philosophical style, the humanities and the academy, genocide, and the ethics of language. Most recently, he has focused on the Holocaust, and has been called "one of the most intelligent of the philosophers who over the past decade have been dealing with the Shoah." His most recent books include: *Writing and the Moral Self*, *Act and Idea in the Nazi Genocide*, *The Anatomy of Philosophical Style*, *Writing and the Holocaust*, and *The Future of the Holocaust: Between History and Memory*.

David B. Morris has written numerous essays and five books, including two prize-winning works on British literature: *The Religious Sublime* and *Alexander Pope: The Genius of Sense*. His highly acclaimed book *The Culture of Pain* (which won a PEN prize), as well as over twelve published essays and numerous lectures on the subject of pain, have earned him a reputation as an expert on pain. He has held fellowships from the Guggenheim Foundation, the National Endowment for the Humanities, the American Council of Learned Societies, and the National Science Foundation, among others, and has lectured to numerous medical and non-medical audiences. His most recent book is entitled *Illness and Culture in the Postmodern Age*.

Roger Shattuck, a fellow in the American Academy of Arts and Sciences, has written, translated, and edited numerous books over the course of his distinguished career, including *The Banquet Years; Marcel Proust*, which won the National Book Award; *Forbidden Knowledge: From Prometheus to Pornography; Candor and Perversion*; and *Proust's Way*. Recently retired as University Professor at Boston University, Shattuck has also taught at Harvard, the University of Texas at Austin, and the University of Virginia.

Preface

The essays in this book were developed from lectures given in a series, entitled "The Question of Evil," organized by the Institute for Advanced Studies in Culture (formerly, and at the time, called the Post-Modernity Project) at the University of Virginia in the Spring of 1997. Selections of some of these essays first appeared in the Summer 2000 issue of *The Hedgehog Review: Critical Reflections on Contemporary Culture*, published by the Institute for Advanced Studies in Culture. Roger Shattuck's essay, "Great Faults and 'Splendidly Wicked People,'" first appeared as "When Evil Is 'Cool'" in the January 1999 issue of *The Atlantic Monthly*.

Acknowledgments

Special thanks are due to James Davison Hunter, the Executive Director of the Institute for Advanced Studies in Culture, who made it possible both for the lecture series to take place and for this book to come into being. Thanks are also due to Kristine Harmon for the copy-editing skills she brought to bear on the pages herein and to Sarah Crawford for her work on the index. Charles T. Mathewes, a scholar well-acquainted with the vast literature on the topic of evil, was of immeasurable help in framing this book and its introduction through the many "evil" conversations we had over the three-year period during which this book was in the making.

Introduction

Jennifer L. Geddes

Evil after Postmodernism

What is evil after postmodernism? Is there such a thing as evil after postmodernism? And if so, how has postmodernism changed our ways of thinking about and experiencing evil? Two extremes mark out opposite ends of the terrain within which the essays of this book navigate their explorations of these questions. On the one hand, there is a fundamentalism that does not shy away from labeling the other "evil," and therefore deserving of any violence that might come his or her way; and, on the other hand, there is a relativism that refrains from making any moral judgements whatsoever, either out of fear of offending someone (or anyone) or out of apathy, a kind of bland tolerance towards everything. Both extremes avoid the difficulty of grappling with evil after postmodernism: fundamentalism by thoughtlessly applying the term "evil," moral relativism by thoughtlessly discarding it. On the one hand, "evil" is a useful word for justifying violence, and, on the other hand, it is a useless or unwanted word. In both cases, a thoughtful consideration of what it might mean to call something or someone evil, what might be achieved and/or lost by such a categorization, remains unexplored. This book attempts to navigate between these two extremes without falling prey to either.

Related to these two extremes in the use of the word "evil" are two opposing views of the relationship between evil and postmodernism. According to one view, there has been so much violence associated with the word "evil," particularly as it has been used by political and religious fundamentalists to justify their aggression against others, that we would do better to be rid of the term. According to this view, the word "evil" is seen as a holdover from metaphysical and religious vocabularies that have been revealed by postmodern thought to be oppressive, binary, totalizing, and exclusionary. The word "evil" should be discarded, it is argued, because it has been used so often in oppressive ways. The act of identifying something as evil, of naming it "evil," actually promotes suffering, and in no small part by continuing ways of thinking that lead to violence and destruction. Many of the events of the twentieth century most often described as evil have been fueled by the indiscriminate (or perversely discriminating) application of the label "evil" to people unlike the perpetrators. The word has been used so often to justify cruelty and violence, is so laden with its historical abuses, so outdated, so metaphysically and theologically burdened, and inextricably linked with the very atrocities it describes, it is argued, that we would do well to jettison it from our vocabulary. If the book championed this view of the relationship between evil and postmodernism, it might well be titled *Postmodernity and the Limitations of "Evil."*

According to the other view, articulated by those who focus on the moral relativism that is widespread in our postmodern world, it is not the case that postmodernism reveals the dangers and baggage associated with using the word "evil," but rather the opposite: that the reality of evil reveals the shortcomings of postmodern thought. Postmodernism, it is argued, has few resources with which to respond to the occurrence of evil, few resources which might guide one in making moral judgements. Its focus on play, on dissolving grand narratives and foundations, on deconstructing binary oppositions, on transgression, leaves it more open to championing (or, at the least, allowing) evil than to preventing it. Evil after postmodernism, it is argued, becomes aestheticized as transgression, as excess, as sublime, and the real sufferings of the victims of evil become eclipsed. Faced with the necessity of responding to the injustices and suffering caused by evil events and actions, we need to be able to identify evil and judge it, and postmodern thought is powerless to do so. Following this viewpoint, the book might become *Evil and the Limitations of Postmodernism.*

Does postmodernism show us that the word "evil" should be discarded from our vocabulary because it is too weighted with metaphysical baggage? Does the occurrence of evil present a stumbling block to postmodern thought, a reality that its theories cannot take into account? Can thinking about evil after postmodernism resist the extremes of fundamentalism and moral relativism?

This book wagers that it can. In between the extreme view that the word "evil" should be left behind and the opposite view that postmodern thought should be discarded, the essays in this book explore the possibilities for thinking about evil with all the complexities that the world after postmodernism presents. While we live in a postmodern world, the movement "postmodernism" has lost the place that it once held. We are now at a short distance from postmodernism and can begin to evaluate its resources and its limitations. None of the contributors to this volume is willing to dispose of the word "evil," but each has something to say about the deficiencies of our current understandings and uses of it. They point out ways in which the word "evil" has been used to justify horrifying events and increase suffering and argue for a better articulation of what we mean by it. Likewise, none of the authors is quick to discard postmodernism: some aspects of it are criticized, while others are seen to be helpful in responding to the particular forms that evil takes in our postmodern world. The essays take upon themselves the more difficult task of seeking resources in postmodern thought for rethinking and responding to evil and pointing out ways in which the experience of evil challenges postmodern thought.

The essays in this book explore the ways in which cultural, institutional, and technological changes have shaped our understanding of what evil is. Because we live in a time of rapid cultural transformation, the ways in which we think about moral questions are also undergoing rapid change. How, with the waning social currency of traditional moral vocabularies, are we thinking about and responding to moral questions? Specifically, how are we thinking about events and situations that have traditionally been described as evil, and how are we thinking about the very concept of evil itself? What is evil after postmodernism?

Writings about evil generally fall into one of two categories: theoretical or empirical. That is, they usually seek either to explain how and why evil things happen in the world, thereby taking up the subject of evil at a conceptual and theoretical level; or they seek to describe and analyze particular events or situations deemed evil. This volume seeks to bridge the divide between these two approaches to evil, combining the strengths of both to overcome the limitations of each. While the theoretical approach explores important questions about the ways in which we think, judge, and understand the world around us, it is sometimes so abstract that the discussion seems to have very little to do with the real suffering of those who are the victims of evil. Evil becomes a problem for thought, rather than a problem of lived experience. This is often the case with philosophical and theological books on "the problem of evil" or theodicies, which attempt to explain or justify the occurrence of evil and to reconcile it with the existence of an all-good, all-powerful God. While these studies offer important clarifications of terms and concepts with which to work, they can be overly theoretical and divorced from the particularity of empirical events.

Conversely, while the empirical approach draws our attention to particular evils that occur in the world around us, it sometimes does so with an underdeveloped understanding of what it means to call something evil. It also easily overlooks the ways in which conceptual frameworks contribute to the perpetuation of evil. Books on evil can be so deeply involved in the description of a particular historical event that they do not move from its specifics to thinking about the larger questions about evil that it raises. This focus is often necessary for the purposes of a book, and historical accounts provide us with important details about atrocities that have been committed and keep discussions of evil grounded in the lived experience of evil. However, books on evil of this sort may not move beyond these details, and more is needed to confront the problems that evil raises.

In gathering the essays for this book, an attempt has been made to counter the limitations of these two ways of approaching thinking about evil by bringing together the concrete and the theoretical. Taking up some of the conceptual and theoretical issues associated with evil in the context of particular, historical, empirical situations, this volume offers strong challenges to, and interesting developments of, current thinking about evil. Attempting neither to explain evil, nor to solve "the problem of evil" that has vexed theologians for centuries, nor to discover something like the essence of evil, the book instead presents a collection of approaches to thinking about evil as both a problem for thought and an aspect of our lived experience. The book draws on the strengths of numerous disciplines – including philosophy, sociology, religious studies, literature, medicine, and history – and this interdisciplinarity serves to resist the narrowness of investigation exhibited by other studies of evil that have emerged from a single discipline. Implicit in this collection is the assumption that such a multi-disciplinary approach is necessary to the task of confronting evil after postmodernism. Because it is interdisciplinary, empirically grounded, and theoretically sophisticated, it is hoped that this book will appeal to a wide range of scholars and students, as well as anyone else interested in thinking about evil in the postmodern cultural arena.

Histories, Narratives, and Ethics

The theme of this volume – evil after postmodernism – and the particular ways the authors have chosen to ground their discussions of it point to new ways to begin thinking and asking questions about evil. The essays are organized around three themes – Histories, Narratives, Ethics – with each theme exploring one area of questions raised by a consideration of evil after postmodernism. The Histories section focuses on continuity and fragment-ation: Is evil after postmodernism the same as evil before postmodernism? What do we do with the fragments of moral vocabularies and cultural narratives that the deconstructing efforts of postmodernism have left us? Is the suffering that took place in the past in continuity with the suffering that takes place in the present? The Narratives section looks at the ways in which narratives shape our understandings of, and responses to, evil and suffering: How should we read stories that glamorize evil? How does the way in which we tell stories about suffering actually increase that suffering rather than alleviate it? The Ethics section explores the difficulties of making moral judgements in a postmodern world: How do our new technologies and increased media presence affect the ways in which evil is carried out and justified? How can we judge something or someone to be evil without falling into the totalizing oppositions that postmodernism has helped us to locate?

Histories

In "Evil Inside and Outside History: The Post-Holocaust vs. the Post-modern," Berel Lang argues for thinking about evil within a context of historical continuity and suggests that the Holocaust be viewed as occurring within a history of evil, rather than as rupturing that history. He attempts "a reconstruction, close to a genealogy, of the moral sense of direction of postmodernity" as a way of looking at its resources for responding to evil, particularly to the events of the Holocaust. Lang finds connections and continuity between the pre-Holocaust and the post-Holocaust, between the modern and the postmodern, in the existence of a moral history, a history of evil.

Larry D. Bouchard explores the question "Is the Postmodern Post-Tragic?," suggesting that the question is about our times and terms and one that implicitly asks: Are witnesses to suffering and evil in our days in continuity with others, past and future? Can terms like "tragedy" or "the tragic" continue to be resources for understanding and critical explanation? Can the category of the tragic still be used as a framework for responding to evil in postmodernity? In response to these questions, Bouchard discusses three theatrical presentations, arguing that "when works of art are juxtaposed, without proscriptive regard to period and style, they can create unusual spaces for attention and reflection across cultural differences." He argues that discontinuity and the juxtaposition of fragments can create space within which thinking about evil can occur.

Narratives

In "Narrating Evil: Great Faults and 'Splendidly Wicked People,'" Roger Shattuck cautions us about the dangers of narratives of evil, arguing that they sometimes translate evil into something that commands our fascination and admiration rather than condemnation. The postmodern translation of evil into the more positive term "transgression" signals, he suggests, a dangerous fascination with evil. He draws on the narrative resources of Diderot, Hawthorne, Baudelaire, Dostoevsky, and Chekhov, as well as the writings of Pascal, Rochefoucauld, Johnson, and Emerson, to caution against applying our intellects to condoning evil. What is most disturbing about narratives representing evil, according to Shattuck, is the variety of ways in which they lure us into seeing a sort of greatness in evil.

In "The Plot of Suffering: AIDS and Evil," David B. Morris looks at how our cultural narratives of suffering and disease, specifically of AIDS, often serve to increase, rather than alleviate, the pain and isolation of those most in need. He suggests that we rethink our narratives of suffering and disease, specifically of AIDS. Morris argues that our personal narratives of suffering are embedded within larger social narratives: "the public discourses of distinct, historical communities shape and constrain how we talk about suffering, how we talk when suffering, and ultimately, how we suffer." Persons with AIDS are thrown into "a net of tacit meanings and subliminal narratives," which tend to victimize them rather than support them in their struggles with the disease. Viewing suffering as embedded in events, situations, and relations resists a static view of suffering that can lead to inaction and hopelessness and pushes for an exploration of its causes and consequences.

Ethics

In his essay "The Reflexivity of Evil: Modernity and Moral Transgression in the War in Bosnia," Thomas Cushman argues for a sociology of evil grounded in a theory of agency, for looking at evil as a form of social action. Though evil has traditionally been "sociology's *Doppelgänger*, always present, but unwelcome, haunting the discipline and its quest for Enlightenment by calling to mind questions of metaphysics, agency, and the 'dark side' of human progress," the events of the twentieth century call for a sociological grappling with the term. Cushman focuses on the self-presentations, through the medium of the Western media, of four Serbian elites who were the principal architects of the destruction of Bosnia: Slobodan Milošević, Radovan Karadžić, Ratko Mladić, Zeljko Raznjatović. His essay reveals the disturbing ways in which the media coverage of, and Western response to, the war in Bosnia contributed to the atrocities committed there, and points out the ways in which evil sometimes gains the mask of decency.

In "Others and Aliens: Between Good and Evil," Richard Kearney explores the ethics of our encounters with others and calls for a critical apparatus that allows us to see behind the mask of evil that Cushman identifies. Using the word "other" to refer to an alterity worthy of welcome (hospitality) and the term "alien" to refer to our experience of alterity associated with hostility, Kearney asks: How do we know whether the stranger at our door is a person in need or a murderer in disguise, a person to whom we should show hospitality or a person whom we should resist? He argues that we need the resources of both desconstruction and hermeneutics: the former to resist prejudices and the temptation to demonize anyone unlike us and the latter to make informed judgements about good and evil. Kearney brings together "an *aporetics of hospitality* represented by Derridean deconstruction" with "an *ethics of judgement* inspired by Ricoeurian hermeneutics." Kearney explores the ethics of our encounters with others – some of whom we welcome as guests and others whom we expel as evil aliens.

Conclusion

We live in the context of a global, multicultural, rapidly changing world; our networks of meaning are many-stranded, loosely woven, and subject to change. We are thinking about evil in the context of multiple worldviews and the practices that follow from those views, and we are learning more and more that there are cultural logics other than our own, and that what may seem to us to be an evil practice may appear quite different to those who live within its cultural narrative. With this increasing information about and contact with other cultures comes an increased opportunity and responsibility both to reconsider our own judgements as to what constitutes an evil action or practice and to evaluate the practices with which we come into contact. At times, there are situations in which we find ourselves morally compelled to intervene in situations that seem to us evil. A global world requires responsibilities of the global citizen that extend beyond the boundaries of his or her neighborhood or nation.

Here, however, difficulties arise: By what criteria can an element of a culture be judged evil by someone from outside of that culture? What does it mean for a Westerner to call female circumcision, or mutilation, or modification (your word choice here reveals your point of view) "evil"? What might it mean for a non-Westerner to describe the practice of male circumcision as child abuse? Might it be necessary to make cross-cultural moral judgements of events that seem to us evil? Are such judgements always morally imperialistic? What sorts of action, if any, appropriately accompany such judgements?

Some would argue that even if such judgements are necessary, we lack the resources to make them – the simple reason being that our inability to judge something to be evil extends not simply to events in other cultures but is as true for events in our own culture. This inability stems from the fragmentation of narrative communities in our own culture. The loosening and intermingling of communities which once had particular narrative identities, drawn from a history of grappling with important questions, has depleted our resources for thinking through and responding to evil. The stories by which many of us make sense of the world are often drawn from several traditions, creating numerous eclectic mixes that may combine the pick of many crops, but may also lack the cohesiveness and richness of a tradition that takes the form of a dialogue that continues over centuries.

In his book *The Death of Satan: How Americans Have Lost the Sense of Evil*, Andrew Delbanco argues that currently images of evil are abounding – as objects of fascination as much as of horror – while our resources for responding to evil are diminishing. For Delbanco, this situation has created a cultural crisis, "because evil remains an inescapable experience for all of us, while we no longer have the symbolic language for describing it."[1] Jean Baudrillard suggests that we in the West have already lost both the word "evil" and the understanding of the world that accompanied it. We are unable to speak the "language of evil," because we have lost the moral frameworks and vocabularies by which such a language would make sense, and instead, Baudrillard argues, we live under a tyranny of consensus, the constraint of toleration.[2]

Concomitant with this diminution of moral vocabularies, and perhaps because of it, evil has become an object of aesthetic fascination, rather than moral concern. Evil has taken on a glamorous sheen. The increasing popularity of horror and sci-fi movies, media attention on serial criminals, interest in the Gothic, the theatricalization of war as it is occurring, to name a few examples, suggest that our culture has a growing obsession with evil. These popular representations of evil tend to relegate it to the realm of the mysterious, the other, and at times, the non-human – in each case, to a realm beyond rational consideration. By being aestheticized, evil has become at once domesticated and removed from the arena of thoughtful concern, and we the viewers of such evil become anesthetized such that our questions take the form of curiosity, rather than concern.

The essays in this book seek to move us beyond either helplessness or anesthetized fascination in the face of evil. They also seek to keep us from thoughtlessly applying the term "evil" to anyone who does not follow our accepted codes of behavior, does not look like us, or threatens our understanding of the world. They call for an engaged and thoughtful response to the horrors of our world, arguing that we need to draw on many resources in order to avoid the temptations that evil presents to us.

Notes

1 A. Delbanco, *The Death of Satan: How Americans Have Lost the Sense of Evil*, New York, Farrar, Straus and Giroux, 1995, p. 224.
2 J. Baudrillard, *The Transparency of Evil: Essays on Extreme Phenomena*, trans. J. Benedict, London, Verso, 1993.

Histories

1 Evil Inside and Outside History

The Post-Holocaust vs. the Postmodern

Berel Lang

On being invited to write about "Postmodernity" and "The Question of Evil," my first reaction was puzzlement. Surely, I thought, a typographical error had crept into this plain and sober formulation. "*The Question* of Evil?" Aren't a pair of scare-quotes missing here – that all-purpose defense against the menace of referentiality which would hedge those two words or at least the too-definite article, in this way blunting the severe implication that there is only one such question and that one self-evident? And then, also, what are we to say about the supposed object of "The Question?" For "evil" is as antique an item as any in the well-stocked museums of ideology, a relic freighted with moralistic lumber carved biblically from that one-of-a-species Tree of the Knowledge of Good and Evil. If postmodernity could be expected to leave anything behind, would it not be just the nostalgia for the binary or dualistic thinking which here opposes virtue to vice and then asserts that we can (and so, of course, ought to) tell, and retell, the difference between them?

Or perhaps, again, the slip might have been slighter, but also subtler and more inclusive – this, in the omission of a question-mark at the end of the title which would have posed "The Question of Evil" as a question itself ("The Question of Evil?"), in this way invoking the same reflexivity that postmodernity typically and liberally demands of others. Or then, turning to the other title in the conjunction, we might well ask about the odd nuance of the term "Postmodernity" itself as it consciously displaces the more common "Postmodernism." The difference appears to be between the contingency of Postmodernism – like any "ism," implying agency, the freedom to join up or to resign (as in Socialism or Buddhism or Impressionism) – and the fixity of the other, that is, the condition indicated by the "ity" ending which, notwithstanding the postmodern suspicion of facts without tears, denotes just such facts (as in "mortality," for example, or, for that matter, "fixity"). And is it indeed the case that postmodernity is the "condition" we are in, and *that*, whether we like it or not?

Puzzling as these reflections were, however, I caught myself before going further, reminded that, after all, typography is not destiny, that what appear to be lapses often turn out to have reasons (whether good or bad) behind them, that on the most basic rule of interpretation, we ought first to suppose that there was intention or deliberation in this title too. And that only if these remedies proved ineffective should moves in other directions be invited. The same cautionary spirit suggested, furthermore, that we look at "The Question of Evil" as postmodernity itself *first* looked at it, in contrast to reading backward to it through the baroque superstructure more recently built on it; that is, to consider "The Question" as postmodernity found it *before* going postmodern – in this way, also learning something of why it decided on that career in the first place.

The framework to be proposed here, then, is in part a reconstruction, close to a genealogy, of the moral inclination or direction of postmodernity. Obviously, even with our own proximity to postmodernity's divorce from modernity (it is difficult to say exactly when this occurred, but it can't be long past), the lineage remains conjectural, although no more, I should argue, than conceptual genealogies ever are and, in any event, no more than the categories of "modernity" and "postmodernity" themselves. A view of them *as* historical will in any event level the playing field, if it does not make it quite transparent. Nor is the issue at stake a history of the development from one to the other as that "actually" occurred, since I shall be attempting only to place them against a common background of moral history or more specifically, the (at least, *a*) history of evil.[1]

It seems to me clear that any attempt to describe a connection among these several factors from the vantage point of the present must sooner or later address the event of the Holocaust, or so consciously avoid it as also to address it: that extraordinary design for genocide which, whether or not it is unique, whether or not (more moderately) it was unprecedented, occludes the view, certainly the *progress*, of twentieth-century history and, more generally, of any moral (and so also, immoral) history that does not simply avoid this century altogether. For Lyotard, the Holocaust defines the break between modernity and postmodernity as a moral chasm marking the end of one and the beginning (less tendentiously, the onset) of the other.[2] This is a dramatic view of the role of the Holocaust within history in general, perhaps as far as one can take it without placing the Holocaust outside history altogether. And it is indeed to stress this limitation – the place of the Holocaust *within* history – that the present discussion is directed.

I mean to argue, in other words, that notwithstanding, or more precisely, because of its moral enormity, the Holocaust is none the less to be registered and understood in empirical and historical terms. In such terms, it appears as distinct, on the one hand, from metaphysical or theological or any other "transcendent" categories; on the other hand, from the bottomless ambiguities and sequence of ironies by which postmodernist ethics (the phrase itself seems an oxymoron) has typically fettered itself. The approach here considers first what stands on the two sides of the Holocaust; that is, the line which marks off the post-Holocaust from the pre-Holocaust as that roughly parallels the related distinction between modernity and postmodernity, and as both those historical "moments" can be viewed in a non-extra-moral sense; that is, morally. My thesis is that far from marking a rupture of or within history, the Holocaust is open to, indeed demands historical, and so also morally historical, analysis and understanding. In other words, it must be placed in an historical field that joins its pre-Holocaust antecedents to the post-Holocaust aftermath. Indeed, the Holocaust as an event provides notable evidence for the claim of this continuum which can thus also be read as a moral history or, less benignly, in a phrase I have introduced elsewhere, as part of a "history of evil." Certain evidence for this claim (as in an example cited below from Primo Levi) takes an unexpectedly commonplace form, although this "alltäglich" quality itself, I hope to show, adds weight to the argument for a moral continuum within, not outside history, and so opposes the claim for the end of one history and the beginning of another, quite different one. In contrast to assorted apocalyptic views which claim that true history begins only when our own nominal history ends (here postmodernity shows vestiges of its modernist predecessors like Marx), the history of evil offers no such hope of reprise or redemption. We find ourselves now *in* that history as we have also inhabited it – although with a difference – in the past. On this view, the intensity added by the Holocaust serves itself as evidence for continuity rather than for rupture, disputing also the diluted version of the "irreversible" break that Jürgen Habermas finds there as he strives mightily to sustain the *pre*-postmodern project; that is, the ideals of the Enlightenment.

To view the traditional question of evil in its original terms is also, I believe, to invite the conclusion just stated, however one otherwise judges the premises of that question. For the question in its classical context asks quite simply how evil is possible – that is, given the divinely or morally-ordered world in which it supposedly occurs – and yields the (also simple) answer that evil is *not* possible. As there are different versions of the "The Question," so also there have been variations on this response, but the common core among them is clear. This is that, however one otherwise analyzes or depicts an event like the Holocaust, in the end, for "The Question of Evil," even that extraordinary instance of moral enormity makes no difference. And this possibly startling conclusion follows for one or both of two reasons. The first of these is that the Holocaust makes no difference for "The Question of Evil" because that question in its traditional setting does not depend at all on the size or scope of the evil involved, on its duration or the extent of its consequences. When we recall Dostoyevsky's challenge to God's justice on the basis of the single tear of an innocent child, we confront the large issue of theodicy in brief: Why, if everything happens for the best, should that single tear be shed? And for this question, the addition of millions of tears (or millions of lives) alters nothing. Without a justification for the one, there can be none for the other; and by the same token, to find a ground for the one would also assure a basis for the other.

The second sense in which the Holocaust does not change anything significant in the traditional response to "The Question of Evil" is this: that given the premise of a morally ordered universe, evil has at most only relative or apparent standing. All local occurrences (that is, historical events) must be judged in the context of the whole. That whole, furthermore, (by hypothesis) has justice or the Good or God on its side – which means in turn that when all has been said and done, it is better to have things the way they are than otherwise, with the implication then, that whatever is judged evil is only apparently so. In these terms, evil as such is also only apparent, at most a privation of reality (as the Platonic tradition has it), at its least a failing of human comprehension to grasp the totality of which humanity's limited comprehension is itself part; human events thus occur on a cosmic and transcendent stage, with the wings of that stage spreading well beyond history. Evil is not actual or real; it is thus historical only as a "likely story" (in Plato's phrase) – a variety of fiction and thus provisional, a station on the way to a larger truth, which journey only demonstrates further its own insufficiency.

In reference to an event like the Holocaust, the implausibility of this view seems especially stark, but we cannot ignore the fact that it has the weight of significant traditions behind it. For the moment, however, its role here is to mark out one position on the map of moral history which I'm sketching and which thus sets this one boundary at the denial of that history's possibility. This denial surfaces not only on a cosmic level, furthermore, but also in a related feature of the human domain. For a side-eddy in the rejection of the notion of a history of evil argues also against the notion of human perfectibility, and thus against a moral history even in respect to human history alone. So, for example, the doctrine of Original Sin asserts the moral finitude of human nature – and the non-metaphorical point of that doctrine is constant and unforgiving even in its more moderate versions, as in the "evil impulse" described in the Hebrew Bible or through the concept of the body as the prisonhouse of the soul asserted in classical rationalism. On these views, since there is no hope of escape from the limits cited, there is also little to say about the detail of their disclosure or indeed about any other incidents or acts in our common experience; what might otherwise constitute a moral history amounts here to only a recitation of episodes, a virtually random chronicle; any apparent pattern is no more than that of a constant present – proof of what is already known and what, under the aegis of eternity, has no significance. Just so, in the Biblical account, we hear a reason for the creation of Eve after Adam – but none, before that, for the creation of Adam himself. (Could what is omitted here have been the *first* bet that God made with Satan – on the basis of which He was later so confident of winning his bet in the Book of Job?)

A second moment in the reconstruction of the history of postmodernity against the background of the Holocaust goes like this: Explanations of the Holocaust's occurrence have moved between two poles. At one of these – one which draws still on the first moment referred to above – the Holocaust is also (still) placed outside time and causality. In one such version, it appears as a fit of national madness in an otherwise rational German history; in a second, quite different version, it appears as an instance of divine retribution for failings on the part of the victims; in the largest number of such accounts, it is viewed as simply inexplicable or (in related tropes) as incomprehensible or ineffable. By contrast, the opposite pole of explanatory attempts replace transcendent explanation with historical explanation. All these attempts include reference to the most obvious historical feature of the Holocaust's temporal and spatial location – the fact that it occurred, after all, in post-Enlightenment Europe, in the Europe of modernity, in one of the centers there of the high culture nourished by that humanist and liberal project. And "The Question of Evil" as it is in this way forced to be historical asks about that new setting in which it is found: Why and how is the connection between the two possible?

This question itself, admittedly, faces a charge of circularity, as it first juxtaposes two events and then asks how that juxtaposition is possible. But the writing of history is inevitably a matter of historians lifting themselves (and their histories) up by their own bootstraps (the hermeneutic circle here bridging the past and the present), and there is, at any rate, no shortage of responses to the question itself. There is the evidence, for one thing, in the Enlightenment ideals of universality, addressed to pure and practical reason (that is, in both science and ethics) and positing also an essential and common human nature. These essentialist dispositions leave little room for any except the most superficial differences or particularity of individual commitments. Followed to their extreme, these principles yield conclusions that by now have become only too evident in the varieties of tyranny and totalitarianism which are all the more menacing in their exclusions or repression because they act in the name of truth. Admittedly, associating the Holocaust with such basic principles of modernity runs the danger of the "post hoc, ergo propter hoc" fallacy; it ignores the possibility, for example, that the Holocaust represented a reaction *against* the modernity project (that would be a very different sense of "propter"), and there is no doubt that much of the Nazi rhetoric, at least at its manifest level, was directed against the Enlightenment's social principles of equality and liberty.

Notwithstanding these qualifications, the evidence seems to me compelling of the "filiation" of principles central to Enlightenment ideals and to the "Emancipation" they heralded as those same principles later surfaced in practices of exclusion and domination; as the latter became embodied in nationalism and racism, they characterized the "totalitarian democracies" of which Jacob Talmon spoke[3] and left signs of their presence even in the more liberal and non-totalitarian democracies. Adorno and Horkheimer's *Dialectic of Enlightenment* advances an extreme version of this view, but its central objection to the abstraction in Enlightenment claims of universality – the assumption in such claims that the universality asserted not only goes beyond all particulars but supersedes and dislodges them, in effect leaving them no place at all – is, it seems to me, compelling.[4] This is not, it should be clear, a claim of "No Enlightenment, No Holocaust," but few historical explanations ever purport to find necessary conditions for the events they explain.

Even a qualified version of this causal relation, furthermore, would provide a justification for the turn from modernity to postmodernity, with that turn then a reaction against the ideas dominant in the former. In this sense, the Holocaust would indeed represent a rupture marking the end of modernity as justified in principle, with history and ethics for once acting there in concert. And indeed, even if the syntax of "postmodernity" inscribes it as a "condition," in the way that I earlier suggested, its advocates have been much more involved with marshalling objections *against* the universalism of the past it claims to supersede than in considering what is alleged to be its accomplishments (for example, the advance in moral history in the modernist discourse of universal human rights). But this discourse is by no means tied to the political or social principles that conduce to the exclusion or denial of particularity, notwithstanding the *historical* link of such principles to the Enlightenment. Thus, the search for an alternative might rest on this very ground: the possibility of legitimizing differences among individuals or groups without precluding the possibility of likeness or trans-personal principles that hold notwithstanding those differences.

The danger in the postmodernist reaction against such universal principles is the familiar one of throwing the baby out with the bathwater. What I propose in contrast is thus meant, in relation to both the "post-Holocaust" and the "postmodern," to save the difference between baby and bathwater and so also to save the one without the other. An alternate way of describing the need for this revision is by noting that although the Enlightenment pitted itself against the obscurantism and superstition of religious or metaphysical thinking that imagined it could reach beyond history, it seems itself in the end to embody a similar impulse. For reason in the abstract, as Voltaire or Diderot or even Kant conceived of it, functions quite apart from any (and so also, it turns out, from every) instantiation; only so, it seems, can we understand the antipathy of these figures to parochialism or (in Kant's term from his essay on "What Is Enlightenment?") to "tutelage" of any sort, even, presumably, if *its* consequences were uplifting or enlightening. In other words, the effort to displace whatever was claimed as transcendent turned out to produce another version of the same; like the other, it too was a- or even anti-historical. Scoffing at Pangloss's naive faith in this "best of all possible worlds," Voltaire himself espouses an optimism on behalf of the power of reason which seems not much different; certainly it nourished in Voltaire, at least as much as it did in Pangloss (or Leibniz), an antagonism to particularity which in retrospect was at once ominous and prescient: I refer here (for one example) to his antisemitism and most immediately to his promise of a "holocaust" for the Jews in that very term (in his *Philosophical Dictionary*). In this way, the turn to modernity, which, after all, had anticipated postmodernity by reacting vigorously against the grand narratives of its past with their transcendent and universalizing impulses, fell victim to the same a- or anti-historicism of those accounts. In respect to their *origins*, the history of modernity and postmodernity are very much alike – a fact which both of them have been eager to obscure or ignore.

The difference between them, then, must be found not in their origins but in their futures, with the future of postmodernity remaining at this point still (to some extent) open, poised between two main alternatives. The first of these would be to declare an end, well-earned and well-deserved, to modernity, marking a breach in history accentuated by the claim that in addition to the human agents responsible for the moral breach, the writing of history itself has been also at fault. For the same "totalizing" impulse that expressed itself in political action, in the "total" state and then also in the Nazis' "Final Solution," would also express itself rhetorically in the total or grand narratives for which typically there was not simply *a* beginning, middle, and end, but *the* beginning, middle, and end. The reaction against that principle then insists that for postmodernity, the units of discourse must be so small and discrete that they exclude, or more strongly, give the lie to, any efforts to place them in a larger narrative, to view them as pieces of a whole. The purpose of this tactic is to break the lockstep of standard historical discourse without, however, losing the force of historical narrative. Also this option, however, whatever its intentions to the contrary, seems to me to place certain events, as well as everything that falls under the heading of values, outside of history; certainly, in the absence of any pattern of relative connectives – causal, temporal, comparative – there would be no historical ground or order among them.

The alternative that I propose here to the postmodern conception of a rupture in history is to view the evidence of history – the same history – as attesting to a kind of filiation or linkage among historical events, including also and even the Holocaust, in such a way as to allow (and then, of course, to compel) us to speak of a moral history, as well as of a causal or explanatory material history. Certain historical events can undoubtedly be described apart from any reference to moral history, not only as an exercise in abstraction but also because the latter is not especially relevant (the Industrial Revolution might be a possible example of this, but even that only until one begins to fit it into the general framework of technology and the relationship of humans to nature). And certainly its place in moral history is as central *historically* to accounts of the Holocaust as any of the other aspects; indeed one can imagine that moral history without the others more readily than one can imagine the converse.

The claim cannot be developed as fully here as it deserves, but I would begin that justification by repeating my earlier assertions about the retroactive status of the Holocaust; that is, with the historian himself as moral agent, responsible for the account he reaches back to in the past, and with the representation of the past then part of a continuum and, in a perverse sense, of a progression. What I mean by this point can be stated in quasi-figurative terms. It would by now require a radical thought-experiment to conceive of a world from which the murder of individuals is absent, whether in fact or idea. Yet it is also evident that there would have been a point in human history when that was the case; we might think of this emblematically through the Biblical account, as the interval between the expulsion from Eden and, subsequently, Cain's murder of Abel. Viewed thus, individual murder would, in Cain's hands, have the character of an invention, a new stage in the progress of evil (following the first, comparatively innocent transgressions of disobedience and then deception in the Garden).

In a similar sense, I mean to suggest, genocide marks a further stage in the same progression, designating the murder not of individuals but of the group *qua* group, including individuals but including them through their identification with the group and then also (or rather, first) requiring the destruction of the group. Considered from this perspective, the concept of genocide not only designates individual historical events (like the Nazi genocide against the Jews), but also inscribes itself as a new element – no less indelible than the earlier ones – of social and moral consciousness. The features of this phenomenon, moreover, are recognizable only in relation to its historical place that is, in respect to what is found or can be imagined on the two sides of the Holocaust: the difference between the pre-Holocaust and the post-Holocaust consciousness. (Whether the Holocaust was the first full instance of genocide has been debated, and I do not judge that question here; the crucial point in this context is that the Holocaust *is* an instance of genocide, and that as such it is also currently emblematic of that phenomenon.)

Viewed under the historical and moral category of genocide, the Holocaust thus expands moral consciousness by its power of invention or imagination (grotesque terms in that context, but there seems no way of further reducing them); but more than this, reflection on the Holocaust also, it seems to me, forces the viewer *into* history – in contrast to leaving him in the role of by-stander, which is what "understanding" by itself might allow. One basis for this contention can be found in the relation of language to the Holocaust, beginning with the term "genocide" itself, which we know emerged from the Holocaust, coined (in 1944) by Rafael Lemkin most immediately in reaction to the Nazis' "Final Solution." Lemkin himself did not claim that the Nazi genocide was without precedent – but he did find that, at the time, there was neither a vocabulary nor a codification of laws applicable to that occurrence. Thus the need for the term "genocide" in order to indicate its distinctive intention and consequences – and so also, in the realm of law, the UN Convention on Genocide of 1948 to which Lemkin subsequently contributed. The term and charge of genocide are so common in current discourse that it would be difficult to imagine a world from which they were absent. It is all the more pertinent, then, to recall how recently they have entered our consciousness and contributed, as they have, to the shaping of moral history and, as I suggest, to a history of evil.

Another means by which moral history is embodied in the issue of Holocaust language is through an absence rather than a presence. This is the fact that even fifty years after the Nazi genocide, no adequate term has yet been found or agreed upon for designating the people who were held and then almost invariably killed in the death or concentration camps. For the Nazis, these people were sometimes "Stücke" or "Figuren" – "pieces" or "figures" – terms typically reserved for things, inanimate objects; in more benign moments, they were for the Nazis "Häftlinge" – prisoners. When the camps were liberated, beginning in late 1944 and then in 1945, the headlines of *The New York Times* spoke about the "slaves" discovered in them who were still alive. But the first pair of these terms – "Stücke" or "Figuren" – are indictments of the speakers who use them. And the second and third of those mentioned are, more simply, false: "prisoners" implies a penal system of *some* sort, with procedures of judgement and punishment, at the very least of a prison intended to contain or keep the prisoner – and "slaves" implies that it is the labor these people provide which is a condition of their existence. But the people in the camps had neither of these behind or before them. Their "prison" was not meant to "keep" them; they had no more rights within than they had outside it – that is, none; nor were they even slaves, since it was at least as much their death as their labor that was expected of them. The people in the camps devised the term for themselves of "Ka-Tzetnik" – from the initials KZ of the "Konzentrationslager," and this is quite precise. But it also lacks descriptive connotation that would place its reference in any more general moral or historical context. In respect to *this* concept, then, the search for language adequate to the Holocaust forces us to address history in the present, and not only to observe or register the past. The inadequacy of language in relation to this or other terms bearing on the Holocaust might seem itself an argument for viewing the Holocaust as a rupture in history, insofar as it reflects an event *still* beyond the reach of language. A likelier conclusion, I believe, would hold that we are forced here to imagine and then to name the agents and elements in another stage of an historical progression which, although exceeding known terms and concepts, gains in intensity from just those terms; that is, through the detail – in this case, the menace – of history itself.

Much more would need to be said on theoretical grounds to elaborate the reasons for locating the Holocaust on an historical continuum that, with the addition of its own distinctive contribution, constitutes a history of evil. But this is, again, a continuum, not a broken line or rupture; a single history, not one which has been shattered and which now has to start over again, beginning with its newest fragment. This point seems to me to be made clearly and graphically in what on the face of it is a commonplace episode recounted in Primo Levi's memoir of his year in Auschwitz. If it attests at once to continuity for Levi between the pre- and the post-Holocaust (and so also, as I would add, between modernity and postmodernity), it detracts nothing from the enormity of the Holocaust or from the challenge posed by that event to the standards of ethical conduct, wherever they appear on that continuum.

In this part of his account, Levi reports on an "interview" he had in the camp with a German chemist, Pannwitz, who was in a position to appoint Levi, also a chemist by training, to his laboratory and so to a job which would to some extent protect him from the worst conditions in the camp. At the conclusion of the interview which, as things turned out, gained him the job and probably his life, Levi is led back to the camp by the Kapo, Alex, who had brought him to see Pannwitz and must now escort him back:

> Alex enters the scene again, I am once more under his jurisdiction. . . . Here we are again on the steps. Alex flies down the stairs: he has leather shoes because he is not a Jew, he is as light on his feet as the devils of Malabolge. At the bottom he turns and looks at me sourly as I walk down hesitantly and noisily in my two enormous unpaired wooden shoes, clinging on to the rail like an old man. . . . To re-enter Bude, one has to cross a space cluttered with piles of cross-beams and metal frames. The steel cable of a crane cuts across the road, and Alex catches hold of it to climb over: Donnerwetter, he looks at his hand black with thick grease. In the meanwhile I have joined him. Without hatred and without sneering, Alex wipes his hand on my shoulder, both the palm and the back of the hand, to clean it; he would be amazed, the poor brute Alex, if someone told him that today, on the basis of this action, I judge him and Pannwitz and the innumerable others like him, big and small, in Auschwitz and everywhere.[5]

Certain features of this incident are likely to elicit immediate assent in the reader. The most obvious of these is that compared to other goings-on in Auschwitz at the time (including other experiences recounted by Levi), this one is negligible, hardly worth mentioning. We hear about the swipe of a hand in a setting of gas chambers and crematoria. A second point, however – at angles if not counter to the first – is the ready recognition of what Levi finds wrongful in Alex's slight motion: not only wrongful but brutish and terrible, with all these terms extending farther than the fact that Alex had soiled Levi's camp uniform. Is it not reasonable to say that what speaks here, what sits in judgement – for us the readers, as it did also in the midst of Auschwitz for Levi – is a post-Holocaust consciousness? One which for him, as writer, recalls the incident and reinscribes his initial reaction – and which for us, now, ratifies that inscription. And can we not also conclude that, however intense they were or are, neither of these reactions differs in its ground from what we recall or imagine as affective in pre-Holocaust moral consciousness as well? Far from marking a rupture in history, in other words, what is evident in Levi's reaction and now, also, in ours, would be unintelligible if not for the linkage it assumes to ordinary (that is, also pre-Holocaust) experience. Here too, it seems, a piece of modernity's moral stance (and pre-modernity's as well) imposes itself on postmodernity – even as the latter speaks now with the voice and authority of Auschwitz. For the challenge in the Italian title of Levi's memoir (*Se questo è un uomo* ["If [this] were a man"]) is just the challenge of moral judgement as such: the requirements and so also the contingencies that have to be met in order to be human.

In referring to this incident, I do not mean, obviously, to equate genocide with the swipe of a hand; the association here points only at a common foundation which Levi himself suggests. Nor is the reference to such a small-scale event intended to revive conservative or reactionary skeletons which depend on such wisdom as "the more things change, the more they stay the same" or Ecclesiastes' weary claim that there is "nothing new under the sun." It assumes only an immediate recognition and assent – first, to Levi's own reaction to the initial event, and then, in his retelling it – and then an understanding of this commonality through what appears to be the one principle underlying it; namely, that, whether we confront the episode pre- or post-Holocaust, pre- or post-modern, what is wrongful in it – and before this, *that* it is wrongful – is evident: as evident, at least, as the quality of any human exchange or transaction can be.

Is the larger implication to be drawn from this small incident indeed the claim that nothing in moral history ever really changes, that we're condemned in moral conscience to a version of the eternal recurrence – although, as it happens, to a version of that cyclical view of history to which its most articulate advocate, Nietzsche, might have objected? Is it, in other words, no more than a revival of the old-time model of good and evil, now additionally burdened with all the standard "other-worldly" baggage? But I have already granted – more than that, claimed to show – that moral history does have a purchase in fact no more doubtful or tenuous than other historical modalities – *and* that the Holocaust figures largely in this history just because of the changes it introduces there. This emerges, however, only as we view that history historically, placing the Holocaust within history, not outside it – and finding it together there not only with modernity but also – however reluctant its appearance – with postmodernity itself. Why should postmodernity be rudely pushed into this position that it has worked so ardently to escape? In the first place, because the post-Holocaust has provided no basis, at least none that does not seem only arbitrary or ad hoc, for claiming a split in history which might then point to *post*modernity as a novum; and then, still more conclusively, because postmodernity does not offer any more compelling evidence or explanation of its own.

Does this mean that there *could* never be an end to this or to any of the many other histories whose obituaries have recently been so prominently announced? Consider only the notable "ends" – of ideology, of art, of politics, of science, of philosophy, of history itself.[6] Why not then also, at the extraordinary crux of the Holocaust, an end to *moral* history – and so too the beginning of something else quite different? To be sure, the very profusion of such announcements, in concert as it were, rouses a certain suspicion: Might this group of supposedly independent discoveries be evidence rather of a fashion (that is, of a *style* of postmodernity)? And then, too, there is other pertinent and historical evidence about such claims which, as it turns out, have been made time and time before. Hegel, for example, proclaimed the end of art almost two centuries before Danto – and the predictions of the demise of philosophy as such have been so common and frequent that Etienne Gilson would find space for a pun to fit the crime. So he considers the long line of philosophers who proclaimed the end of their history (invariably, of course, as a result of their own achievements): "Philosophy," he notes, "has repeatedly buried its undertakers."

Lines of demarcation of all sorts have a certain attraction, if only that of the taboo. This allure in general would be further heightened by the prospect of living transcendently, outside history, of positioning oneself beyond the particular history that is declared to be over. But in shrugging free of the past in this way, we are also obliged to imagine what a future without it will or could be; this is much more difficult to do, although not necessarily as a deficiency in the imagination. I think here once more of Nietzsche, undis-puted as a herald of the postmodern, who having himself left good and evil behind, having transvalued all values, none the less, on that fateful day in June 1889, which marked the beginning of what would then be his own eleven-year ending, when he saw a cab driver beating his horse, ran across the Square in Turin and flung his arms around the horse's neck before then collapsing. Was that act, *is* it, so difficult to understand as a response to brutality or cruelty? Do we, in order to understand this reaction, require new moral categories based on the displacements of postmodernity that would then supersede those of modernity? Or can we not rather infer a certain continuity, a grasp by the past on the present that extends also (or at least) to ethical response and judgement, that links the two in terms of principle as well as of practice? Titles or rubrics are, to be sure, the least of the matter, but on these grounds, "*trans*modern" or "transmodernity" would seem to have at least as strong a claim as "postmodern" or "postmodernity."

Hoping to find consistency between the postmodern Nietzsche and the impulsive gesture of a broken but morally driven man, between the Levi of Auschwitz and the survivor dwelling on a memory of the swipe of a hand, we might prefer to conclude here that like politics, all ethics is local, *only* local – "alltäglich," perhaps also "allmählich" (gradual). On such a view, it is not principles, whether moral *or* historical, that would then be at issue, but only individual moments of decision and design: no grand narratives, only simple or partial and, in any event, small ones. Most advocates of post-modernity have indeed urged conclusions of this sort. But I do not think in fact that such conclusions can or ought to be the moral of the hopefully moral (or morally hopeful) story recounted here. For one thing, this inference runs into a straightforward problem of logic: How could one justify ruling out (a priori, as it must be) the possibility of general moral principles, however time-worn they (or we) are by the time they are considered? And still more pressing than this is the historical evidence that does indeed point to the existence of a moral history (that is, ethics within history), disclosing there a texture of continuous threads or filiations, a woof as well as a warp. There is no denying the omnipresent temptation to think apocalyptically, of hoping somehow to manage to jump out of one's skin. *Either* that – or, at the other, anti-apocalyptic extreme (no less apocalyptic), the lure of individualism, of the autonomous self (that is, body): the hope that we may someday, somehow, become *all, and only*, skin. History is at times disjointed, often even shattering. But sometimes, too, among the fragments by which it reveals itself, it also, despite itself, discloses continuity and what *look* like recurrences and constants. Admittedly, even when these appear, they provide no explanations of their occurrence – and often the explanations then summoned from the outside have occasioned more, and sharper, reactions than the first appearances themselves.

Perhaps then it is the *desire* for explanations of the moral continuum that is the problem, not the constant failure to find them and the new pangs of conscience that such failures then add. Why not, after all, start with what we know, at least with what we *act* as if we know? For finally, in moral judgement, even for the role in that judgement of the moral imagination, it is in the end what we do that at once judges and is judged by us. As a conclusion, this modest proposal may not seem much of an advance for either postmodernity or the post-Holocaust. But then it may be salutary to recall, in the same deflationary spirit, that there is ample precedent for this, too, in the past – that such advances as had been made before them were also piecemeal and small, also anticipated, even begun in what had come before them. Post-Holocaust understanding, then, is in this sense pre-Holocaust understanding. Only more so.

Notes

1 For a fuller account of the concept of the "history of evil," see B. Lang, *The Future of the Holocaust: Between History and Memory*, Ithaca, Cornell University Press, 1999, chs 1–3.
2 See J.-F. Lyotard, *Heidegger and "The Jews,"* trans. A. Michel and M. S. Roberts, Minneapolis, University of Minnesota Press, 1990.
3 J. Talmon, *The Origins of Totalitarian Democracy*, New York, Praeger, 1960.
4 T. W. Adorno and M. Horkheimer, *Dialectic of Enlightenment*, trans. J. Cumming, New York, Herder & Herder, 1972; see also on this issue B. Lang, *Act and Idea in the Nazi Genocide*, Chicago, The University of Chicago Press, 1990.
5 P. Levi, *Survival in Auschwitz*, trans. S. Woolf, New York, Collier Books, 1959, p. 78.
6 On the prospect of such "ends," see, e.g., D. Bell, *The End of Ideology*, Glencoe, IL, Free Press, 1960; A. Danto, "The End of Art," in B. Lang (ed.) *The Death of Art*, New York, Haven Publishers, 1984; A. Schedler, *The End of Politics?*, New York, St Martin's Press, 1997; J. Horgan, *The End of Science*, Reading, MA, Addison-Wesley, 1996; M. Heidegger, "The End of Philosophy and the Task of Thinking," in *Basic Writings*, trans. J. Stambaugh, New York, Harper & Row, 1977; F. Fukuyama, *The End of History and the Last Man*, New York, Free Press, 1992.

2   On Contingency and Culpability

Is the Postmodern Post-Tragic?

Larry D. Bouchard

Is the postmodern post-tragic? The question is both about our times and about our terms. It is not a new question, having been posed often since the Second World War and probably since Nietzsche, depending on when one thinks modernity began to end. Must we be stuck with these words, "modern," "tragic," and "post"? Might we merely treat the query as a riddle, whose answer is: "Probably so"?

When, however, the question is posed seriously – when it asks whether witnesses to suffering and evil in our days are in continuity with other pasts and futures – then the question may help us respond to some of the fragments of art and testimony we encounter. The question simply asks whether "tragedy" and "the tragic" will continue to be resources for understanding and critical explanation.

Although these terms resist essential definition, I generally reserve "tragedy" for a family of interrelated artistic forms. It includes Greek and Elizabethan tragedy, certainly, but extends to other forms and works that are "in dialogue" with the traditions of tragedy. "The tragic" will stand for the kinds of questions and experiences that tragedy poses and probes. Tragedy as art, then, is better defined not in terms of what it is but what it does. Among the things it does is inquire.[1] Tragedy stages questions of suffering and evil so as to elicit communal inquiry. Later I will reframe these questions in terms of configurations of "contingency" and "culpability." If tragedy speaks appropriately to postmodern times, it may well be in its witnessing and inquiring into such configurations.

Juxtaposing Fragments

To so distinguish between "tragedy" and "the tragic" allows us to better ask about how art both shapes experience and raises questions about it. So another way to pose our opening question is to ask whether tragedy, as a family of art forms, continues to help us identify, probe, and make urgent the ways in which evil and suffering are related in our late time. Does "tragedy," in other words, still explore "the tragic"? Yes, I want to say, it does. And yet, how may one even speak now of the relations between suffering and evil, when "suffering" is what postmodernism better comprehends, after the shared narratives that underwrote the meanings of "evil" have fragmented?

These questions are obviously contingent upon the times in which we pose them. And they depend especially upon the sense of fragmentation felt in the cultural spaces we know. But if we take the metaphor of cultural fragmentation seriously, we need to consider whether our questions do not also depend upon what actual fragments – of historical experience and culture, of literature and art, or of philosophies and religions – happen to come in view at the times of our questioning. Thinking that the particular fragments make a difference, I will proceed shortly to a kind of travelogue of three plays showing in London in September 1996. These plays will serve two purposes: as candidates for "tragedy" and as illustrations of a practice fairly common in postmodern reflection, i.e., the method of both making and recognizing juxtapositions of contingently related texts or practical situations before proceeding to more systematic theory-making.

The fact that anyone might compose a travelogue of artworks arranged side by side – that is, juxtaposed but not tightly fused together by theme, period, or artist – has a bearing on my approach to questions of contingency and culpability. The performances that came to be arranged, despite their differences, were self-consciously "postmodern." They each embraced some putative aspect of postmodernity: the imperative of self-critique; the worried embrace of "otherness" as an ethical claim; and the mixing of periods, styles, and cultural forms in art. Individually and together, they reflected their location among the theatre-going publics of 1990s London and other European cities. And except for the civic themes in the Oedipus plays, these performances did not urge the conservation of cultural and religious identities – another crucial trait of postmodern times. So while this juxta-position opens spaces and paths for thought about the tragic, it does not foreclose other spaces that may open later and elsewhere.

Why should we look to art for space to think together in times of fracture? It is commonly understood that a work of art or literature often juxtaposes the familiar with the strange. The result may be a creation of new meanings and audience responses – be they harmonious, dissonant, or fragmentary responses. It is less commonly considered how works of art are also juxtaposed with each other: in an artist's life work; in museums, galleries, concert halls, and theatre centers; on home bookshelves and office walls; in places of ritual and worship; and especially in classroom syllabi. Those are the places where we usually find art, not isolated but in proximity with other works. That is, part of how we commonly experience and under-stand art is as fragments of tradition, history, and reflection set in juxta-position.[2]

A juxtaposing of fragments demarcates a particular space and time. Between what is juxtaposed, there is set aside time and space to enter. In this time and space, we can attend, read, or even perform these works and converse together about them. It is not only a matter of enjoying the new meanings or resonances that the coinciding works occasion – as when *Oedipus the King* is read alongside Strindberg's *Dream Play* or Freud's *The Interpretation of Dreams*. It is also a matter of the opportunities for sustained reflection that their coming together offers. We enter the space and time they set apart, and their semantic or emotional harmonies and dissonances start extending into our conversations and debates, and – if we ourselves are artists in any sense – eventually into our own aesthetic making. In these spaces, we may find ourselves responding to and participating in communities of thoughtful festivity, which traditionally accompanied all the arts and the performing arts in particular.[3] A literary or artistic tradition, in fact, can be imagined as a pattern of such juxtapositions, which lives over long periods of time but remains subject to growth, decline, re-ordering, and change. We can think of tragedy this way and also of the entangled experiences of suffering and evil, contingency, and culpability that tragedy helps us identify as "tragic."

Travelogue

At the National Theatre, specifically in the Olivier, which mimics a Greek amphitheatre, Peter Hall directed Sophocles' Oedipus plays, *Oedipus the King* and *Oedipus at Colonus*. The actors' individually molded masks and the rhymed iambic pentameter English text (commissioned from Ranjit Bolt) were played so as to intensify the contrast between the formality of move-ment and language and the extremes of emotion. Hall intended that the masks "liberate" the actors. "Although they hide the face, masks open new areas of those who wear them."[4] So the masks renewed old questions of how artistic forms can both contain and catalyze an erupting exposure of trauma, in selves and in communities. And they also renewed questions of how the mask or the theatrical or social role – far from something to "hide" behind – may be a form through which an agent may realize a new direction for identity. Masks, these icons of ancient theatre, can signify both the constructed character of selves (we *are* the masks we are given culturally and socially) and belief in the authenticity of individual expression (we wear our own masks to make our own meanings) – themes that remain in tension in postmodernity.

The masks were also intended to provide a disciplined way of expressing overwhelming sorrow and astonishment. On the set for *Oedipus the King*, we saw the filthy, exhausted population of Thebes crouching before the towering doors and intruding platform of the King – with coal fires burning for warmth and for the removal of human and animal detritus. This tableaux of fatigue and plague (which in destroying fertility denies Thebes its future as a society) must have invited many of us to juxtapose issues of disease, embodi-ment, and exile with the politics of HIV, for instance, and quite possibly of genocide in the Balkans and central Africa.[5]

By contrast, the music and set of *Oedipus at Colonus*, with its bright aluminum surfaces, were a clean and calm transformation of the first set.

They served to call the first play and the first questions into new questions, into new reversals. Who is Oedipus now? This man whose identity has been problematic since birth, who in the persona of King came to know himself to be strangely accountable for his own and Thebes' suffering, now understands himself to be an innocent sufferer. Now at the end of his days, another community – Athens – embraces him, this outcast and scapegoat, as an effective sign of its own security. And yet, when Oedipus rejects the entreaties of his exiled son Polyneices, we remember that the politics of dismemberment will continue in *Antigone*, the later story that Sophocles had written much earlier. The tragic requires yet resists final aesthetic containment.

Across the river, The Royal Shakespeare Company mounted a six-hour version of Goethe's *Faust*, Parts I and II, in a black box theatre at the Barbican Centre. The production appealed to a wider range of theatrical tastes and interests: in eroticism, voyeurism, forbidden and violent knowledge, metatheatrical magic, and real fireworks. The show continually risked going "over the top" – which it had better if 200-plus pages of Goethe in free English verse were to hold us rapt for such a span. And they did.

What makes the end of *Faust* hard to play today is its "happy ending." Unlike Marlowe's, Goethe's Faust is redeemed at the last second, which, near the century's close, could hardly be to anyone's taste. For much of what seems unredeemable about modernity arguably owes something to the Faustian imagination, which in the twentieth century was enlarged through technological power and bureaucratic efficiency. Faust's fascination with "excess," writes Roger Shattuck, "constitutes a problem or a paradox not so much because it afflicts a few unstoppable figures that traverse our lives and our history, but because the rest of us have a hard time not admiring even its most monstrous forms."[6] However, such admiration can pull us up short, and when we do recognize something of Faust in a Stalin or Hitler, we may find we are not in an admiring mood. Faust's redemption cannot be played – unless, that is, we can ironically recognize and enjoy *Faust*'s trick of provoking us to admire or forgive ourselves. And that may have been the tactic of this production.

At first it seemed the show would end with Faust's death, as Mephistopheles looks on – an utterly vacuous death, for Faust has admitted to having reached a kind of stasis. He has possessed and put aside every pleasure he could imagine and, now blind, believes he has attained an image he wishes to fix forever in time.

> Oh, I say
> To this fleeting moment,
> You are too beautiful,
> Stay.[7]

With that last, static desire, Mephistopheles wins his bargain. As Faust lies inert, the music suggests that this is indeed his end. . . . Then, suddenly, the

"Poet" rushes frantically on stage to confront the "Director" with the fact that this is not the proper ending, this will not do, we must play the text as written, etc., etc. So the "Director" reluctantly has the actors restart the last scene, whereupon lovely angels descend on flying trapezes to save Faust's soul. His salvation was burlesqued. God was rolled in as an old man in a wheelchair. The heavenly ones had fluffy wings with gold tinsel and wore white diapers. They spoke chorally, upliftingly, as profound horns and celestial violins played oh so loud – and all this as a trapeze lifted Faust happily as high into heaven as the very low ceiling would allow.

And we who saw it felt something of uplift ourselves – but what did our recognition mean? Was it that in laughing at Faust, we were justifying ourselves, saying knowingly that we know we cannot play the ending any other way, that we know Faust cannot be forgiven because the horror of our century cannot be, but we at least can delight in this knowledge? Is that how we pardon ourselves? Or, rather, was our laughter also the laughter of practical resistance, laughter in the face of Faust, the laughter that refuses to be choked by history, the kind of grim angelic laughter Elie Wiesel's Stranger (given by another the angel-name Gavriel) embodies in *The Gates of the Forest*? Or was our laughter confessional – a way of acknowledging the perplexity and the confusions we continue to have about moral culpability and the contingencies of history and social circumstances, and about how we might be implicated in faults that are not in any simple way "our fault"? Are we responsible for Faust, or to the tradition that bears his name? If so, through what modes of accountability?

At another of the theatres at the National, on a proscenium stage transformed into a kind of shadow box or giant *camera obscura*, was performed for eight hours *The Seven Streams of the River Ota*. The Ota flows through Hiroshima, and the play was a collaborative piece by a Quebec company called "Ex Machina," led by Robert Lepage. Its own streams follow the story fragments of survivors and their descendants, through Europe, New York, and Japan. From the American occupation of Japan in 1946 into our own near future, their lives become entangled by chance encounters and subsequent histories. The players performed in several languages – French, German, English, Czech, and Japanese – and the production incorporated its own translation through supertitles and actors playing interpreters. It also used a variety of media and vehicles, including Japanese Gagaku music, photography, film, a scene from a farce by Feydeau, and video to convey what amounted to, if you will, a postmodern morality play.

To simply state the issues and actions juxtaposed in *The River Ota* is to risk the offenses of mere enumeration. Nevertheless, it is clear that contemporary obsessions with identity and gender were placed adjacent to stories of death complicated by love. Mirror imaging was one of its motifs. In New York in 1965, two brothers named Jeffrey, separated all their lives by circumstance and nationality (one Japanese, one American), narrowly miss discovering together their fraternity upon the death of their father – who in 1946 had been an American GI assigned to photograph the damages of Japan and who made love to a *hibakusha*, an atom bomb survivor. In 1985 the American Jeffrey, who has contracted AIDS, goes to Amsterdam to marry – not so much for love as for the right to commit legal (because he marries a Dutch citizen) physician-assisted suicide. Thereafter Ada, his widow, goes to Japan to meet an older Czech woman, Jana Capek, who as a girl knew Ada's mother, who in 1943 committed suicide at Terezin. Eleven-year-old Jana escaped, only because a stage magician smuggled her out of a Nazi deportation center, using mirrors, a suitcase, and sleight of hand. It is through Jana's narrative that the whole play is framed. She has emigrated to Japan to learn Zen Buddhist compassion and detachment, and now tells us,

> To cut the ego with the sword is the ultimate combat. *The Seven Streams of the River Ota* is about people . . . who came to Hiroshima and found themselves confronted with their own devastation and their own enlightenment. For if Hiroshima is a city of death and destruction, it is also a city of rebirth and survival.[8]

And we, the audience, were invited to enter these spaces of compassion and detachment. Five intermissions and a break for supper insured that very few of us wanted to leave early. We enjoyed a long afternoon and evening at the theatre and its environs beside the river in London.

"After" Tragedy and the Tragic?

Now, having demarcated, with our travelogue of performances, a space for reflection on our terms and our times, let us return to our opening question: Is the postmodern post-tragic? I can think of at least three kinds of reasons for saying "yes" – yes, ours is a post-tragic time, and hence the paradigms and very terms of tragedy are probably inappropriate signs.

First, we might follow those who caution that literary "tragedy" is a closed genre no longer capable of important innovation; if we attempt to repeat this genre, the results will be pale and distracting imitations of, or posturing toward, tragedy.[9] Of the London plays, only *Oedipus the King* unambiguously "fits" the traditional genre. *Faust* is hard to classify even before the redemptive ending turns it into a quasi-Christian comedy. And to define *The River Ota* as tragedy requires further reconception of the genre. While some of its story fragments resemble modern naturalistic or social tragedies (such as Strindberg's, Ibsen's, or Arthur Miller's), *The River Ota*'s eclectic spectacle comments on the limits of theatrical drama itself – although, its length does recall the Greek convention of a tetralogy (three tragedies and a satyr play) performed in the course of a single day.

Or, second, we might aver that "the tragic" usually has reference to religious or mythical views of suffering and evil that no longer obtain. They no longer speak to us, either because reigning Western religious traditions have taken us "beyond tragedy,"[10] or because after modernity the mythic or religious traditions needed to sustain tragedy no longer reign.[11] "The tragic" and even "evil," by such views, may be essentializing categories properly left only to antiquarian interests. The staging of *Faust* directly announced this skepticism with its burlesqued finale. In the Oedipus plays, Peter Hall's use of masks and iambic pentameter challenged us to appreciate aesthetically and socially the possibilities of an utterly remote mythic and ritual tradition. And the emptying of the cremation urn at the end of *The River Ota* may have signaled an ill-defined, persistent desire for ritual ordering, a desire commonly denominated as "spiritual."

Or, third, we might judge that tragedy and the tragic have been eclipsed by the historical traumas that our century in particular has witnessed. By this view, literary tragedy never imagined genocide of such proportions and regularity; in our time, history has been far more efficient at imagining evil than art has been.[12] To denominate genocide and the ensuing rupture of religious and humanistic structures of meaning as "tragic" would be to impose a form on that which has ruptured form, to project a definition on that which resists defining, to interpret and thus to violate that which defies interpretation. Again, both *Faust* and *The River Ota* address such views more or less directly. *Oedipus the King* was so staged as to wager that we can, however, make some thematic connection between the sense of rupture in our day with the terror of an infertile, plague-ridden Thebes, on the verge of losing its future.

So the postmodern *is* post-tragic? Let us consider again. It is certainly possible, as I have hinted, to counter each of these warnings. One could argue that literary genres are not static forms, but rather pluralistic families of formal resemblance and difference. Some new students of genre would have us say that genres function to help us make art, and do not merely classify art.[13] (This is part of why I said at the outset that tragedy is better defined through what it does, not what it is.) Moreover, genres can change, intersect, and ramify but need not finally close. Old tragedies are newly performed and innovative works, which may cogently be interpreted as tragedies, are still made.[14] Or we might argue that "tragic experience" is not really a falsely essentializing or irrelevantly mythical category but can generate newer questions in continuity with older questions.[15] Or we could simply notice that there are in fact contact points between the fragmentary traditions of tragedy and the kinds of evil and suffering witnessed in our time and the times of our parents and grandparents – contact points we noted in our travelogue.

What all three objections to tragedy suggest is that we are too late for tragedy, or that tragedy is a belated category. To this I want to respond that "tragedy" and "the tragic" have always been belated categories. The "tragic" is, and always was, a "post"-category of experience, discovered in interpretation. Likewise, the forms of literary-dramatic "tragedy" are and always were themselves post-tragic. Tragedy must be at some distance from the experiences it re-presents. At a distance, tragedy might name an experience or give it voice and currency (or else encumber it with inept language or images). Tragedy is and was a constructed spectacle, confession, or witness. Thus, if we think of tragedy mainly as an ideal type by which to classify art, we may well find it inappropriate now. Likewise, if we speak of it as a singular tradition, a fabric without frays, tangles, or seams – much less tears – it will be hard to find the continuities between it and the broken strands of our times, spaces, and lives. But we can think of tragedy pluralistically and heuristically: it can explore varieties of "tragic" experience.

If one defines even Greek tragedy ostensively by the extant plays, one finds a plurality of dramatic forms. As a family of generic resemblances, it includes Euripides' *Alcestis*, which seems to end comically, and *The Trojan Women*, which offers us a descending gyre of grief. It explores figures like Agamemnon and Medea, who commit culpable error, and figures like Oedipus and Aeschylus' chorus of *Persians*, who seem more the victims of divine caprice, fate, or chance.[16] It includes stories of conflicting values, such as those Hegel admired in *Antigone* – moral dilemmas compounded with issues of youth versus age, women versus men, kinship versus *polis*, and the efficacy of ritual versus that of politics.[17] Tragedy comprises not only what Aristotle considered good plays but also bad, like Sophocles' *Philoctetes*, whose grotesque, ulcerated leg and unrelenting anger are resolved by a *deus ex machina*. Today, this play is recognized to be among the more compelling of the Greek tragedies, in part because of its phenomenology of physical pain and social embodiment and isolation.[18] When we think of tragedy as a ragged tradition of innovation, then we can more easily see how the Elizabethans and the moderns are in continuity with that tradition. Tragedy may well have been reinvented on a biblically, as well as classically affected, European stage. And modern dramas of psychological and social realism, and later the proliferation of metatheatrical and metafictional forms, are often critical and ironic responses to the traditions of tragedy.

As to "the tragic," the effects or experiences identified and explored by tragedy (what are called "tragic visions") are also plural and shape our language and perceptions unexpectedly. In ordinary language, how we name experiences "tragic," though often denigrated as trivial, is shaped by the historical sediments of tragic art. Tragedy leaves us with language and images by which we recognize, name, and interpret a variegated range of experiences.

For instance, at the end of Hemingway's story "Big Two-Hearted River," Nick Adams, a young man possibly traumatized by his memories of the First World War, hesitates to go further downstream to fish for trout in a dense and forbidding cedar swamp. Nick considers that "in the fast deep water, in the half light, the fishing would be tragic. In the swamp fishing was a tragic adventure. Nick did not want it."[19] In Hemingway criticism, one finds that the use of "tragic" here is a strange attractor of all kinds of aesthetic, philosophical, and even religious commentary. Is this a story of repressed trauma, or relief from trauma? Is the term "tragic" consistent with a ritual structure overlaying Nick's state of mind while fishing, or is it merely portentous, if not pretentious? The language of tragedy can function heuristically even in our ordinary speaking, as it may for Nick, as a way of discovering and trying on meanings – sometimes definitively, more often provisionally. What purposes might be served by calling the fishing "tragic"? What might be discovered? What might be missed?

In recent years, the tragic has frequently been interpreted under the aspect of *tuché*, a Greek word for chance, luck, or "contingency" – in some contrast to the specters of *moira* (fate or destiny) or of "evil." There are a number of possible reasons for this turn. Fate can sometimes be viewed as less an independent cosmic force than an arrangement of circumstances, like the premises of a good plot.[20] And the origins of culpable evil in Greek tragedy are often entangled with divine caprice and so are crucially indeterminate. Oedipus, for instance, has his faults, but they do not drive the plot or explain his story.

Contemporary interest in contingency in tragedy also comes with a greater appreciation for the inherent limits of language, frameworks of meaning, and systems of thought. One of the more common definitions of postmodernism is sustained suspicion about foundations or "meta-narratives."[21] Tragic contingency correlates with what Martha Nussbaum would have us recognize as the plurality and "fragility" of the various goods that give direction to our lives (e.g., friendship, health, aesthetic pleasure, justice),[22] and to what classicist James Redfield and others describe as the limits of virtue and cultural value, which are explored in tragedy.[23] And recent associations of tragedy with contingency also correlate with a hesitancy to use the term "evil" as a moral and religious category. I would extend these views that tragedy teaches us to reflect on contingency. But I would also invite a return to understanding the tragic not only through the contingencies of life and thought but also in terms of their entanglement with ethical and religious questions of moral culpability.

Contingencies . . .

The idea of contingency evokes a complex range of meanings, ranging from "what is the case but might not have been," to circumstances that accidentally threaten well-being, and even to the sense of unforeseen, surprising realizations of good. The various ways in which contingency and culpability become entangled (but not fused or equated) in tragedy can also evoke a sense of mystery, which may remind us of its association with sacred festival. To the extent that tragedy and religion remain occasions of postmodern understanding and critique, their juxtaposition may continue to provide spaces for exploration. So I propose that tragedy can become compelling to us as it inquires into areas of contingency that bear upon the religious imagination: among these are the *contingencies of mystery, of selves and communities, of suffering and moral culpability*, and of what the biblical traditions might learn to call the *contingencies of grace*.

... of Mystery

In much religious discourse, mystery is a value-laden term, both when mystery is intrinsically valued – as in the mystery of divine election – and when the sources of values and virtues (such as justice, beauty, love, wisdom, integrity) are deemed not amenable to exhaustive or reductive explanation. Mystery corresponds, then, to an awareness of the inherent limits of knowledge, and yet points to possibilities of knowing beyond or within those limits. By contrast, exhaustive, reductive explanation might be a modern value that opposes the very notion of inherent mystery, as when E. M. Forster's Cyril Fielding opines in *A Passage to India* that there are no mysteries, only muddles.

Tragedy may both encourage and chasten our desire to recover a sense of inherent mystery – not so much mysteries to be solved as mysteries that persist. Mystery may occur in some configuration that has surprising relevance for our self-understanding, or mystery may disrupt understanding altogether. The art of tragedy may muddle as well as disclose mystery. It is sometimes said that if Oedipus had simply ignored the fragmentary knowledge he received from oracles, memories, seers, and messengers, his ruin could have been avoided. But not only is it contrary to his nature to ignore such gnosis, his own ruin has already been entangled with that of Thebes – a city for whom his past threatens to annihilate its future. His mystery of origins is, for his adopted citizens, arbitrary, capricious, and finally unarguable. Their configuration in his lot simply *is*, as is his with theirs, and it displaces the conditions for understanding. In postmodern parlance, their near ruin is experienced as a rupture in the world.[24] And the easing of the intensity of rupture, first by the exile of Oedipus and later by his near apotheosis at Colonus, does not finally heal it; for the rupture will continue to ramify in story after story.

Tragedy usually inquires into mysteries that are not welcome. If there is welcome news in this, it may be that tragedy often alerts us to the idea of the "irreducible." To acknowledge that some questions – perhaps concerning the origins of the personality or of a historical catastrophe – are "irreducible" to a single framework of causal or functional explanation is to become open to a sense of mystery that might enrich our awareness of the range of that question. However, we should also say that what we discover to be irreducible is likely to be contingently so. Yesterday, we had no terms for explaining the Sphinx's riddle. Today, Oedipus arrives and answers it. Tomorrow we will send him into exile. Then Freud will come. And so on. Sometimes some compelling question – perhaps of who is responsible for this good or this evil, or a question about the origin of consciousness – appears to us as not reducible to single explanatory strategies. And *while* this particular compelling question appears irreducible, it may well appear deeply so, completely so. But appearances can change with histories of knowing, and can change yet again. The history of oracular knowledge is as contingent as the history of persons. Tomorrow we will know, then we won't, and later we may know again.

. . . of Selves and Communities

If Oedipus has a contingent "self," it is a self thickly entangled with multiple communities and times. Charles Segal and others have charted how Oedipus, throughout his life, was abandoned and found on the borders of nature and culture. [25] If structuralism is itself a story that crosses the frontier between modern and postmodern, it has no better hero than Oedipus. He is as socially constructed a character as we might imagine ourselves to be, and hence as liable to schism or disassembly.[26] Looking back to him, and forward from him, we can recognize the dissolving of the modern, essential self – if that is what we are looking for. Or we can see him as the radically responsible self that we may hope ourselves to be – if that is what we are looking for. And we may witness both sorts of postmodern selves in *The Seven Streams of the River Ota.*

In this piece of epic theatre, certainly no character is an island. Their lives overlap, diverge, and interchange across generations and across seas and continents. No one's language or speech is insular in this play, for Lepage's collaborators dramatize a phenomenon defined by Mikhail Bakhtin, *hetero-glossia*: all our speaking is socially and linguistically inhabited by the speech and language of others.[27] And no character's history is insular, for the fragments of their stories have been configured in the denouement of historical catastrophes – those of the Holocaust, Hiroshima, and the Cold War. However, for all this centrifugal social force, all this dispersion and mixing of characters into boundless relations, times, and places, *The River Ota* is also about the mutual respect and accountability of persons with and for others, known and unknown, in the past and in the future. This play's attempt to account for both the boundless relationality as well as the unrepeatable distinctiveness of persons is not exceptional among stories today. One could cite plays and novels of Tony Kushner and Toni Morrison as comparable examples.

. . . of Suffering and Culpability

The multiple languages and theatrical traditions in *The Seven Streams of the River Ota*, as well as the story of Jana (the Czech-Jewish survivor who adopts Buddhism in Japan) certainly fits the impression that pluralistic culture is fragmentary. To some the stridency of our debates over ethical issues and frameworks signals the absence of any kind of cultural and moral consensus. To others, our shrill arguments obscure what moral agreements we may indeed share, even across the many cultures in our common life.[28] But in any case, it may be quixotic to try to speak of "evil" in our cultural setting. The word is so tradition-laden as likely to be meaningless apart from particular religious or philosophical narratives.

And yet to say that our time is without a sense of evil is at least paradoxical – inasmuch as our century has produced events as recognizably abominable as any history has known. And in some postmodernist commentary, it is the unprecedented magnitude and horrible particularity of these events that occasions the pervasive sense of rupture from past and future I have mentioned. We may argue about whether we are really postmodern now. But the proposition remains compelling that western culture's sense of its own possibilities has been sundered by moral and political catastrophes – those associated with totalitarianism, war, and genocide – events which renew our doubts about the final humaneness of humanity. Perhaps only Greek tragedy's scenes of plague, as in *Oedipus*, or the despair of war and displacement in *The Trojan Women*, invite us to make hesitant comparisons with the eruptions of our time.

However, the mingling of boundless desire with fear, and especially the mingling of knowledge with great power, which has so enlarged our capacities for catastrophe, have indeed been explored throughout the history of tragedy and also of most religious communities. When students of Western religious thought – especially those responsive to Augustine's belief that the *telos* and good of a human being is to reply to love with love – locate places for the tragic, they tend to move along either of two directions. They may consider the moral ambiguities of tragic choice to be ultimately a consequence of sin (forms of misdirected loving, which corrupt the good) or else that sin is a response to tragic suffering and contingency.[29] These two trajectories for understanding the tragic only roughly correspond to the distinction between moral *hubris* and natural evil.

Along the first direction, exemplified by the mid-twentieth-century American theologian Reinhold Niebuhr, the matters we may call the tragic in life (choices, dilemmas, and the suffering that follows from them) are interconnected and inseparable from their sources in prior sin. Here, the tragic includes sin, the psychological and social contexts for sin (e.g., anxiety, temptation, and the historical momentum of injustice), and the kinds of suffering that are the consequences of sin: structures of injustice, oppression, and reciprocal violence. Why is sin prior? For Niebuhr (as for Kierkegaard), our anxieties about the future tempt us to try to secure ourselves against contingency, no matter the cost. Sin, then, is seen as a deeply contradictory motivation to make oneself (or one's group) the infinite center of the world – a *hubris* that inevitably leads to others' (and one's own) suffering. The powerless slave suffers the effects of the sins of slavery; the culpable slaveholders are also slavery's victims. In short, as far back into a history of causes of injustice or resulting suffering as one wants to go, the tragic is a personal and social complex intractably rooted in sin.[30]

Along the other trajectory, exemplified by the contemporary theologians Edward Farley and Wendy Farley, tragic suffering *precedes* sin.[31] The *hubris*, violent hatred, selfishness and greed, rationalized preference and privilege, and slothful resignation that can beset persons and groups are seen as bad responses to conditions of being finite: that is, to scarcity and other natural limits, to conflicting values and goods, and to the pervasive realities of death and pain. By this account, what is tragic in life is the priority of contingency and suffering, not the priority of sin. Sin, rather, is a deeply contradictory response to the tragic contingency. If, in the Bible, the stories of the Fall or the Tower of Babel are images of the first trajectory, whose source is sin, the stories of Job and perhaps of the clinically depressed King Saul are images of the second, whose source is a lack of fit between human well-being and the finite world. I do not claim that these two theological directions for understanding the tragic are mutually exclusive (for the terms are defined and distributed differently) – only that they are different and are not reducible to each other. Culpability and contingency are lines that tangle and cross each other in endlessly ramifying ways. And literary tragedy calls us to respond to particular tragic entanglements of culpability and chance.

From the standpoint of culpability, Faust is the restless, expansive ego who perversely imagines himself infinite. To a weaker man this pretension to "play god" might come to little. Faust, however, receives sufficient power to act upon all his pretensions, and the ruin of countless others follows in his wake. Yet considerations of contingency tell us that the *hubris* of Faust is not sufficient to explain his story, especially when we place it both in its mythological and historical settings. God and Mephistopheles – as in the book of Job – have arranged the circumstances of Faust's bargain, and these supernatural figures suggest a contingent play of necessity and circumstance beyond what Faust (or Job) can pretend to grasp. Further, Faust's story itself is part of the cultural "fate" that impinges on later times. If we resonate with his bargain and understand it well, it is in part because with the images that pass before Faust on stage we can recognize the history that made realizations of this late myth all too possible. What Conrad's Marlow says of Kurtz applies here: all of seventeenth- and eighteenth-century Europe contributed to the making of this Faust. His circumstances appear in an age that imagined the individual to be a point of absolute moral and material reference, while consigning the many to political and economic oblivion.[32]

As far back as one traces the history of sin, Niebuhr and Kierkegaard tried to say, there is prior sin: "sin presupposes itself."[33] Yet as far back as one presses this analysis of sin, contingencies also appear that are not reducible to sin-as-culpability. The complications of sin and historical chance are muddled together as far back as we can see or imagine. And the interpretation of such muddles as occasions of "mystery," with that word's connotations of both awe and perplexity, is among the perennial implications of tragedy. Bernard Williams recognizes that this entanglement of contingency with culpability runs counter to how we usually link moral responsibility to an agent's knowledge and intentions; so, typically, we do not want to hold Oedipus responsible for unwitting actions or forced choices. Indeed, Oedipus interprets his personal innocence in *Oedipus at Colonus*. But Williams' claim is that the tragic view offers a richer and more realistic description of the ethical environment – an environment we continue to probe along with our Greek (and, I would add, Hebraic) ancestors: "As the Greeks understood, the responsibilities we have to recognize extend in many ways beyond our normal purposes and what we intentionally do."[34]

So accustomed are we to treating mitigating circumstances only as reasons for pardon that some may assume that such readings of tragedy can only weaken moral accountability. On the contrary, the coarse mixing of contingency and culpability – which often cannot be sorted out and finally assessed, and which might well define the ethical character of "the tragic" – vastly enlarges our "accountability" – especially as witnesses. We are called to bear witness and become responsive – that is, "to give account" – to the appearing of moral evil implicated in: contingently related structures of nature, visible and invisible historical patterns of injustices, ideological distortion, and suffering.[35] We find ourselves accountable witnesses to such mixes of contingency and culpability in ways that resist *simple* ascriptions of innocence or blame. Consider how, upon discovering Jocasta's suicide and after blinding himself with her brooches, Oedipus addresses the query of the horrified Chorus:

> How? How could you bring yourself to do it?
> To put your eyes out? Which god drove you to it?
> *Oedipus*. Phoebus it was, and only he, that brought this all about –
> Heaped on my head
> This woe. But *my* hand, no one else's, dashed my poor eyes
> out.[36]

The complexity of his considered reply – it was Apollo's hand, yet it was my hand – points toward a kind of "tragic accountability." Before a mysterious convergence of contingency and culpability, which he recognizes but cannot resolve, Oedipus yet finds himself obliged to give an account to Creon and Thebes. And his accounting poses questions of our own accountability as witnesses and interpreters of tragic suffering and evil.[37]

. . . of Grace

After the contingencies of mystery, selves and communities, and suffering and evil, we might ask if it is possible to speak of the contingency of grace. In religious thought, the evocation of grace after an exposition of evil is sometimes called "theodicy," which can mean, as Milton said, to "assert providence and justify the ways of God to man." Today, a number of theologians have stopped trying to do that – justify God and evil – worrying that solving the problem of evil was never the right project, was not even a Jewish or Christian project, but was rather an Enlightenment project doomed to fail.[38] Some have redefined theodicy as "practical theodicy" – where one does not aim to justify God abstractly but to resist the effects of suffering and evil concretely and compassionately.[39] Tragedy in general can contribute to such praxis by its being a form of inquiry, a heuresis and not a gnosis, a way of asking questions and of keeping those questions alive. If grace can mean openings or new possibilities for life together after impasses have foreclosed justice and compassion, then there is the chance of grace in questions. Real questions may come to us as gleanings or gifts, and they may open spaces for things to happen, including – I take it – possibilities for understanding, transformation, and practical resistance.

The Seven Streams of the River Ota ends with the pouring of an urn of ashes into the bay of Miyajima, where the river Ota empties. We remain uncertain whose ashes these are, for the survivors who have gathered near a Torii arch, here, have all lost friends to remember. The closing tableaus of the play define a space for many questions. My first were: Are these images of resignation or resistance? Are the cutting of the ego and the cultivation of detachment and compassion ways of practical resistance or a quiet capitulation to the ruptures the play has evoked? I suspect these were the wrong questions, or at least not the last or best questions, so I need to look for others.

Robert Lepage's theatrical company takes its name from probably the most embarrassing feature of Greek tragedy, the *deus ex machina*, the god from the machine. I do not know why they call themselves "Ex Machina." Connoisseurs of tragedy have usually despised such divine interventions, but there is evidence they are being staged again – and not just in burlesques, like the diapered angels of Goethe's *Faust*. Irish poet Seamus Heaney uses the *deus* in his version of *Philoctetes, The Cure at Troy*. There it reminds us that not all contingencies are harmful and frightful, but that healing can also happen contingently, as can release from impasses of violent hatred and entrenched anger. The *deus ex machina* was despised because it was arbitrary; it broke the formal unities of drama. However, these unities are themselves arbitrary; the fine fabrication of plot, character, and thought is a frazzled texture of arbitration. So the theatrical machine may be a more honest sign of tragedy and art.

Tragedy is a many stranded tradition that lives as old plays are performed and turned into new plays, stories, and works of other arts. The ways we participate in this tradition are fragmentary, and we encounter the fragments in odd and arbitrary juxtapositions. I saw *Oedipus*, *Faust*, and *The River Ota* that week in London, and the three plays worked together. I also saw a good production of *A Midsummer Night's Dream*, and it did not fit with the other three plays. It could have added to that lucky constellation; it did not, but perhaps it may yet. Such arrangements are contingent and temporary. They do not compel us to synthesize what is juxtaposed, but invite us to hold them tentatively as fragments, and think with them and between them, perhaps as we have not thought before. Such arrangements of art open spaces for many futures. When we enter these spaces, we don't know where we will exit. Who will answer the questions that come to us in such encounters? We may have to simply wait – to wait for other fragments and juxtapositions, for other plays and persons, for better ideas than our own. They will probably come, but juxtaposed with other, perhaps devastating ideas as well.

Near the end of *The Seven Streams of the River Ota*, Jana, the Czech survivor who became a Buddhist in Japan, tells how she first came to Hiroshima.

> I believe that Hiroshima chose me. Ten years ago I came to visit a friend and I thought I would find devastation here, but instead, I found beauty. You know, the kind of silence after the storm. . . . And I needed it so badly, I went to the Peace Memorial Park, and I found Prague! There in front of me. . . . It was the only building at the epicenter of the bomb that remained standing . . . and the Japanese preserved it as a symbol of the war. It was designed by a Czech architect, Jan Letzl, who lived and worked in Japan during the twenties. So for me, that metallic skeleton was like being in front of a mirror. This empty shell was myself. Me, with my illusions, and all my past on my Jewish shoulders. . . . So I understood that my place was here, in Hiroshima.[40]

In the play, this speech occurs during the slightly absurd taping of a television interview with Jana, which will be interrupted, rearranged, reshot, and spliced together. There is nothing final about the statement Jana makes. It does not define itself as universal; it does not insist on taking us into its space. Jana does, however, juxtapose persons, art, and history, and in between those fragments she finds a space for compassion and for inquiry. We are invited to enter the space she allows, and with grace we may, or may not – if not this time, then perhaps another.

Notes

1 On how tragedy may be defined as an aesthetic mode of inquiry, with help from Aristotle and recent genre theorists, see my *Tragic Method and Tragic Theology: Evil in Contemporary Drama and Religious Thought*, University Park, Pennsylvania State University Press, 1989, especially pp. 8, 18–23.

2 The metaphor of juxtaposing fragments has many sources, especially in the literature of postmodernism, but also in currents of religious thought. See especially E. Fackenheim's employment of the metaphor in *God's Presence in History*, New York, Harper Torchbooks, 1970, in reference to the writing of fragmentary midrash after the Holocaust. See also D. Boyarin, "Voices in the Text: Midrash and the Inner Tension of Biblical Narrative," *Revue biblique*, 1986, vols 93–4, pp. 581–97. The idea of entering the time and space between works of art (considered as fragments from traditions) is in part adapted from liturgical practice, in which a homilist reflects on one or more scriptural readings specified

for the day by a lectionary. It is also indebted to "reader response" literary theories, in which the text is conceived as a texture of "gaps" that structure or confound the reader's expectations.

3 On festivity and community in the reception of contemporary art and literature, see N. A. Scott, Jr., *The Wild Prayer of Longing*, New Haven, Yale University Press, 1971, ch. 2; and R. Detweiler, *Breaking the Fall: Religious Readings of Contemporary Fiction*, San Francisco, Harper and Row, 1989, especially ch. 2.

4 P. Reynolds, *Unmasking Oedipus: Rehearsing Peter Hall's Production of Sophocles' Oedipus Plays for the Royal National Theatre, May–September, 1996*, London, Royal National Theatre, 1996, eighth unnumbered page past the cover.

5 Throughout the late 1980s and 1990s at National Theatre productions, depictions of group suffering implicitly (sometimes explicitly) commented on the scene just outside, where the path of many playgoers took them past a shantytown of cardboard boxes housing homeless persons sheltered beneath part of Waterloo bridge.

6 R. Shattuck, *Forbidden Knowledge: From Prometheus to Pornography*, San Diego, Harcourt Brace, 1996, p. 105.

7 J. W. von Goethe, *Faust Parts One and Two*, new version by H. Brenton from a literal translation by C. Weisman, London, Nick Hern Books, 1995, p. 266.

8 R. Lepage and Ex Machina, *The Seven Streams of the River Ota*, London, Methuen, 1996, p. 1.

9 On closed genres, see M. Bakhtin, *The Dialogic Imagination*, trans. C. Emerson and M. Holquist, Austin, University of Texas Press, 1981, p. 3; on the pervasive pessimism of modern thought (and, by implication, literature) parading as "tragic" sensibility, see L. A. Ruprecht, *Tragic Posture and Tragic Vision: Against the Modern Failure of Nerve*, New York, Continuum, 1994.

10 R. Niebuhr, *Beyond Tragedy: Essays on the Christian Interpretation of History*, London, Nisbet, 1938.

11 See G. Steiner, *The Death of Tragedy*, London, Faber and Faber, 1961.

12 L. Langer, *The Holocaust and the Literary Imagination*, New Haven, Yale University Press, 1975.

13 See P. Ricoeur, "The Hermeneutical Function of Distanciation," *Philosophy Today*, 1973, 24, pp. 129–41. M. Gerhart develops implications from Ricoeur and others in *Genre Choices, Gender Questions*, Norman, Oklahoma University Press, 1992.

14 For an account of political and psychological rationales for a number of late twentieth-century stagings and transformations of Greek tragedies, see M. McDonald, *Ancient Sun, Modern Light: Greek Drama on the Modern Stage*, New York, Columbia University Press, 1992. The literature on modern tragedy is immense, of course, but a good recent discussion is B. Johnston, "Ibsen's Cycle as Hegelian Tragedy," *Comparative Drama*, 1999, vol. 33, pp. 140–65, which reflects on both the "inutility" of tragedy to pragmatic agendas and the continued pertinence of the genre.

15 After first composing this essay, I encountered W. Storm's *After Dionysus: A Theory of the Tragic*, Ithaca, NY, Cornell University Press, 1998. Storm revisits the association of Greek theatre with Dionysus; the tragic correlates, through the Dionysian *sparagmos* (dismemberment), with divisive forces that make and also unmake characters or selves, physically and especially spiritually. Such forces, Storm argues, constitute the a priori tragic condition that the Greek tragedies, and plays like *King Lear* or *The Seagull*, confront.

16 Culpability in Greek tragedy, even when clearly evident, is itself invariably hedged by circumstantial and supernatural contingencies, such as *até*. See P. Ricoeur, *Symbolism of Evil*, trans. E. Buchanan, Boston, Beacon, 1967; on the *Persians*, see pp. 218–19. On Agamemnon's culpability residing in his failure to lament the

meaning of sacrificing his daughter, however forced a choice, see M. Nussbaum, *The Fragility of Goodness: Luck and Ethics in Greek Tragedy and Philosophy*, Cambridge, Cambridge University Press, 1986, p. 49.

17 See G. Steiner, *Antigones*, New York, Oxford University Press, 1984, p. 231.

18 See E. Scarry, *The Body in Pain: The Making and Unmaking of the World*, New York, Oxford University Press, p. 5; D. Leder, "Illness and Exile: Sophocles' *Philoctetes*," *Literature and Medicine*, 1990, vol. 9, pp. 1–11.

19 E. Hemingway, *In Our Time*, New York, Scribner's, 1925, p. 211.

20 In *Nature and Culture in the Iliad: The Tragedy of Hector*, Chicago, University of Chicago Press, 1975, J. Redfield considers how the meaning of fate in Homer converges with the contingencies of plot, as viewed by Aristotle. In retrospect, a good story seems necessary, it "could only happen that way." But what is "necessary" follows not from any clockwork determinism but from the arrangements of circumstance and plot. These things happened, and they happened this way; they might have been otherwise, but were not: "We are shown, not the pervasive operation of general laws, but the special interconnection of particular significant events" (pp. 246–7 n5).

Drawing in part from Redfield, B. Williams in *Shame and Necessity*, Berkeley, University of California Press, 1993, elaborates on necessity in tragedy, exploring how its source can be in a character's sense of integrity (e.g., "given who I am, could I do otherwise?") and how necessity is not inconsistent with effective action: "[S]upernatural necessity does not in general involve immediate fatalism or anything like it. Sometimes, as in Agamemnon's case [the sacrifice of Iphigenia] . . ., the necessity presents itself to the agent as having produced the circumstances in which he must act, and he decides in light of those circumstances" (p. 139).

21 J.-F. Lyotard, *The Postmodern Condition: A Report on Knowledge*, trans. G. Bennington and B. Massumi, Minneapolis, University of Minnesota Press, 1984, p. xxiv.

22 See Nussbaum, *The Fragility of Goodness*, pp. 3–7.

23 See Redfield, *Nature and Culture in the Iliad*, especially chs 1–2, see also J. D. Barbour, *Tragedy as a Critique of Virtue: The Novel and Ethical Reflection*, Chico, CA, Scholars Press, 1984, and Williams, *Shame and Necessity*.

24 See S. E. Shapiro, "Hearing the Testimony of Radical Negation," *Concilium*, October, 1984, vol. 175, pp. 3–10; A. A. Cohen, *The Tremendum: A Theological Interpretation of the Holocaust*, New York, Crossroad, 1981.

25 C. Segal, *Tragedy and Civilization: An Interpretation of Sophocles*, Cambridge, Harvard University Press, 1981.

26 Here, Storm (*After Dionysus*, pp. 91–4) is particularly relevant for thinking anew the relationships between tragic theatre and character, for – unlike prose narrative – live theatrical performance is grounded in the powers of persons to imitate others, to exchange and discard masks and *personae*, and hence in their vulnerability to others' entrances and exits.

27 Bakhtin, *The Dialogic Imagination*, pp. 262–74. See also M. Harris's discussion of Bakhtin in *The Dialogical Theatre: Dramatizations of the Conquest of Mexico and the Question of the Other*, New York, St Martin's Press, 1993.

28 See J. D. Hunter, *Culture Wars: The Struggle to Define America*, New York, Basic Books, 1991, and J. Stout, *Ethics After Babel: The Languages of Morals and the Discontents*, Boston, Beacon, 1988, for two different views of moral disagreement in contemporary American religion and culture.

29 I examine these directions in "Tragedy, Sin, and Contingency: Trajectories in L. Gilkey's Interpretations of History and Nature," in *The Thought of Langdon Gilkey*, K. Pasework and J. Pool (eds), Macon, GA, Mercer University Press, 1999. When they are sensitive to the wide range of meanings associated with tragedy and the tragic, Augustine-informed thinkers may from time to time move

on both trajectories of interpreting the tragic – as does Gilkey in *Reaping the Whirlwind: A Christian Interpretation of History*, New York, Seabury, 1976, and in *Nature, Reality, and the Sacred: The Nexus of Science and Religion*, Minneapolis, Fortress, 1993.

30 See S. Kierkegaard's analysis of anxiety in *The Concept of Anxiety*, trans. R. Thomte and A. B. Anderson, Princeton, Princeton University Press, 1980, and R. Niebuhr, *The Nature and Destiny of Man*, vol. 1: *Human Nature*, New York, Scribners, 1941, chs 1, 7–9. Niebuhr's view of the tragic should not be identified with the idea of Job's comforters, namely, that God simply wills suffering on persons as just punishment for sin. The view is rather that oppression, self-delusion, and eventually the fall of the powerful are structural consequences of the spiritual dynamic, sin, i.e., the hubristic imagining of infinite power or self-securing autonomy.

  Among feminist theologians especially, this account of sin is criticized for its gender-specificity. That is, it applies best to the hubris of the powerful, who in a patriarchal setting are typically male. In a still widely cited article from 1960, "The Human Situation: A Feminine View," *The Journal of Religion*, vol. 40, pp. 100–12, V. [Saiving] Goldstein urged that sin, to be a meaningful religious category, should include succumbing to the temptation to remain distracted or disengaged, or to fail to resist the expectation that women (and others in society) should nurture others at the expense of their own self-nurture. Here what is called for is greater attention to the culpability of resignation, in contrast to that of inordinate pride or infinite desire.

31 See E. Farley, *Good and Evil: Interpreting a Human Condition*, Minneapolis, Fortress, 1990, especially ch. 6; and W. Farley, *Tragic Vision and Divine Compassion: A Contemporary Theodicy*, Louisville, Westminster/John Knox, 1990.

33 See A. MacIntyre, *After Virtue: A Study in Moral Theory*, 2nd edition, Notre Dame, University of Notre Dame Press, 1984. See also R. Niebuhr's *Moral Man and Immoral Society*, New York, Scribner's, 1932.

33 Kierkegaard, *The Concept of Anxiety*, p. 32.

34 Williams, *Shame and Necessity*, p. 74.

35 See Chesire Calhoun, "Responsibility and Reproach," *Ethics*, 1989, vol. 99, pp. 389–406.

36 Sophocles, *The Oedipus Plays*, trans. R. Bolt, Bath, Absolute Classics, 1996, p. 56, Bolt's emphasis.

37 See my discussion of tragic accountability in *Tragic Method and Tragic Theology*, ch. 6.

38 See W. C. Placher, *The Domestication of Transcendence: How Modern Thinking about God Went Wrong*, Louisville, KY, Westminster/John Knox, 1996; and K. Surin, *Theology and the Problem of Evil*, Oxford, Basil Blackwell, 1986.

39 In addition to W. Farley, Placher, and Surin, see P. Ricoeur, "Evil, a Challenge to Philosophy and Theology," *Journal of the American Academy of Religion*, 1985, vol. 53, pp. 635–50; and M. I. Wallace, *Fragments of the Spirit: Nature, Violence, and the Renewal of Creation*, New York, Continuum, 1996, pp. 189ff. See also my "Holding Fragments: Medicine and Practical Theodicy," in *Pain Seeking Understanding: Suffering, Medicine, and Faith*, M. E. Mohrmann and M. J. Hanson (eds), Cleveland, Pilgrim, 1999.

40 Lepage and Ex Machina, p. 106.

Narratives

3   Narrating Evil

Great Faults and "Splendidly Wicked People"

Roger Shattuck

> . . . that which we call sin in others is experiment for us.
>
> Emerson, "Experience"

I begin with three stories, three moral tales.

*

In late Medieval Avignon, a certain man gains the confidence and warm friendship of a good-hearted and wealthy Jew. The man lives in the Jew's home and becomes his closest confidant. One day, the man comes home in despair. He tells the Jew that someone has denounced them both to the Inquisition, the one as a despicable Jew, the other as a renegade from the only true religion. They will soon be imprisoned, tortured, tried, and burned at the stake. But the man has a solution. The Jew should without delay sell everything he has and charter a fully equipped ship, onto which he can load his fortune. Then the two of them will quietly sail away to safer shores. All these plans are rapidly carried out. Then, during the night before the planned departure, the man rises stealthily, robs the sleeping Jew of his last possessions, and slips away alone aboard the ship with all its treasure.

The events extend to more than a clever swindle. The report about the Inquisition is partially true. For, before escaping, this "friend" denounces his benefactor to the Inquisition and arranges that its agents seize the Jew early on the morning of his own flight. A few days later, the Jew dies horribly by fire. His treacherous friend has come to be known as the Renegade of Avignon.

*

Late at night outside a remote New England village early in the nineteenth century, a lime-burner named Bartram is tending his kiln. Its flame-licked door looks like a private entrance to the infernal regions. Announced by a frightening roar of laughter, the previous owner of the kiln returns after many years' absence. He announces to Bartram that he has found what he set out to seek: the Unpardonable Sin. Where did he find it? The wanderer laughs again scornfully as he lays his finger on his own heart. Some local residents assemble to acknowledge, but hardly to celebrate, their fellow's return, and to inquire of his obsessive quest for the Unpardonable Sin. Strange omens during the evening, such as a dog suddenly chasing its tail, suggest that the devil is lurking in the neighborhood. It is whispered among the guests that the former lime-burner has carried out fiendish psychological experiments on young and old. Left alone finally to attend the kiln for the night, the wanderer recalls that he did not, properly speaking, find the object of his quest. Rather he himself produced the Unpardonable Sin. For in seeking that knowledge, his fierce intelligence separated from and outran his heart.

In the morning, Bartram does not find the returned wanderer. But in the hottest part of the kiln, he discovers an unconsumed piece of marble in the shape of a heart.

*

Living alone in a Paris garret, an idle young bohemian meditates on the sudden perverse spurts of energy that can interrupt a life of laziness and boredom. Such urges lead one to unthinkable acts – like starting a forest fire or lighting a cigar next to a powder keg – just to see what will happen, to tempt fate.

One morning the young man wakes up in a mood to perform such an outrageous action. Seeing below in the street a window-glass vendor, un vitrier, with his stock of panes in a pack on his back, he summons the vendor to climb the six stories to his garret. He asks for tinted glass, which the vendor does not have. In a rage, the young man kicks the vendor back out into the staircase, where the tradesman almost stumbles under his heavy load. Then, watching from the balcony, the young man drops a flower pot just as the vendor appears in the street and thus breaks his stock of glass to smithereens. This vicious prank may damn him, the young bohemian says to himself, but it also has brought him a moment of infinite bliss.

The Renegade of Avignon, the obsessed lime-burner, and the young bohemian in his garret, all display resoluteness in their behavior and consciousness of the baseness of their actions. And one can trace in the narrative voices a mounting fascination with the presence and the problem of evil, an attitude that borders on admiration for it. These three narratives, all very short, cannot aspire to any tragic or epic proportions. Their intimacy, combined with a certain mystery of the inexplicable, gives them the status of moral enigmas.

The Renegade of Avignon is not content to abscond with the good Jew's entire fortune; this traitor, who would be assigned to the lowest circle in Dante's Inferno, also contrives to have his victim burned at the stake. The three-page story appears about half-way through Diderot's widely influential, underground dialogue, *Rameau's Nephew* (1761–74). The parasitic, clowning Nephew half-jocularly and half-seriously cites the tale to show how one can become a "great personage." In this case the Renegade allegedly displays "unity of character" in his sustained viciousness. The Nephew calls it "sublimity in evil" and enthuses over the deeds. His interlocutor, Myself, presumably speaking for Diderot, observes, "I don't know what horrifies me more, the villainy of your Renegade or the tone of voice you use to tell his story."

Many readers will have recognized Nathaniel Hawthorne's story, "Ethan Brand" (1850). This dark tale implies that Brand has done unspeakable things to a local girl and to others, and has come to some understanding with the devil. But the essence of the Unpardonable Sin is neither of these. It lies in the intellectual sin of pride in undertaking the search for the Unpardonable Sin in the first place, even though Brand never intentionally wished to commit the sin. That overweening ambition turned his heart into stone. "Ethan Brand" offers a strong parable of Forbidden Knowledge in which the desired and prohibited goal is to discover ultimate evil. That goal is simultaneously self-fulfilling and self-defeating. The parable addresses all forms of knowledge that can be seen as presumptuous – philosophical, psychological, scientific, even literary.

The young Parisian who gratuitously and fiendishly victimizes a poor glass vendor inhabits the imagination of Charles Baudelaire in one of his prose poems called "The Unfortunate Glazier." These two pages written around 1862 may well have been read by Dostoevsky, whose *Notes from Underground* (1864) reads like a sustained recasting and elaboration of Baudelaire's vignette. Both of them treat characters who approach cruelty and crime as a psychological and intellectual experiment. Cultivating their most selfish impulses, they reach a point of practicing wickedness without a purpose, without a cause. Neither commits a capital crime, but their logic could lead them easily in that direction.

If these tales enlighten us in any fashion about evil, one thing they seem to establish is that evil comes in several forms. The Renegade of Avignon premeditates his theft and his treachery over a certain period of time. He plots both how to obtain the Jew's cooperation in his scheme and how to eliminate the only witness of his crimes. The hideous cruelty of the Jew's death is largely unnecessary, a kind of maestro's flourish or a fiend's laughter. It is the part of the story that the downtrodden Rameau's Nephew finds sublime in evil, demonstrating an enviable "unity of character."

Ethan Brand spends even longer than the Renegade in meditating upon and finally carrying out his immense project of discovering the Unpardonable Sin, the ultimate evil which even the love of God incarnate cannot wash away. Presumably, Ethan Brand believes that his quest for knowledge will serve mankind and will bring him some form of reward and satisfaction for his devotion to a lofty goal. The story has a strong Faustian ring.

But there is more evidence to consider. When Bartram sees Ethan Brand lay his finger on his heart to designate where he found the Unpardonable Sin, the simple lime-burner comes to a conclusion never denied elsewhere in the story. He must be dealing with "a man who, on his own confession, had committed the only crime for which Heaven could offer no mercy." Only after an undescribed point of no return that takes place off-stage does Ethan Brand comprehend that the terrible knowledge he seeks in the world and in other people resides in himself in the form of that very quest. Curiosity and pride blind him until it is too late. The Unpardonable Sinner can now only return to his starting place and destroy himself by casting himself into the inferno that originally inspired his nocturnal meditations on evil.

Baudelaire's bored bohemian neither plots nor sustains any purposeful mental activity. Through absence of meaningful occupation, he becomes the victim of sudden willful actions that seem to serve no personal interest, contribute to no consistent character. The reward he claims is "dans une seconde l'infini de la jouissance." This instant of mental voluptuousness stands for a reverse epiphany, a negative transcendence toward baseness and inhumanity. All of us can and have felt this tug toward what is vile and have yielded to it in varying degrees. The fragile compact we live by declares that we should not follow these impulses too often or too far. Baudelaire did not pool all his resources in order to seek the one ultimate unpardonable sin.[1] He reports in formal verse or in prose poetry on his recurrent encounters with these reverse epiphanies, these glimpses into the abyss. His power as a poet arises from the way his lines create a tensely divided feeling, composed of fascination for evil and revulsion from it. Rameau's Nephew would have found nothing sublime about such an attitude – no unity of character.

Because of their modest length, I have denied to these three tales any epic or tragic dimension. Each one concentrates its attention on a particular form of evil. And that attention in all cases ascribes a strong presence to evil, a perverse stature not reduced or redeemed by any other force in the story. Moreover, the narrative voice and incidental details in each story oblige us to ponder the implied greatness *of* evil – its claim on our admiration as a dynamic element of reality – and an implied greatness *in* the evil of certain dark personages.

In order to deal with this vast subject on a small scale, allow me to leave aside major figures like Milton's Satan and Goethe's clownish Mephistopheles. Instead, I shall comment on three short quotations that may concentrate the matter for us. Two seventeenth-century French authors will go a long way to open the question.

The complete text of one of Blaise Pascal's most troubling *Pensées* runs to four lines:

> Evil is easy, its forms are infinite; good is almost unique. But there is a kind of evil as difficult to identify as what is called good, and often this particular evil passes for good because of this trait. Indeed, one needs an extraordinary greatness of soul to attain it as much as to attain good.[2]

Elsewhere, Pascal has told us insistently that man's greatness resides in his capacity to think: we are frail reeds, but reeds capable of thought.[3]

What, then, is this unexpected and even inappropriate "greatness of soul" summoned from nowhere to explain a particularly rare form of evil? No other *pensée* in Pascal addresses this unusual exception for an undefined variety of evil. Does Pascal envision here a moral-metaphysical mission like Ethan Brand's to search out a special form of evil that can pass for good? Possibly. But there is not enough evidence to guide our conjectures. Pascal offers us a riddle without a solution.

Pascal's contemporary, the Duc de La Rochefoucauld, wrote even more succinctly on the same moral dilemma: "Il n'appartient qu'aux grands hommes d'avoir de grands défauts." ["Only great men can have great faults."] La Rochefoucauld does not write: "The greater the personage, the more destructive the faults." Perhaps that is too evident. Instead, he introduces a pun on the word "great." "Great" can mean "worthy of admiration and respect;" it can also mean, more neutrally, "large in extent, big." "Great men" employs the first evaluative meaning. We admire them. "Great faults" employs the second descriptive, and neutral, meaning. Nothing to admire here. But, by a back-formation, the second "great" is attracted to the first. We end up hearing a certain moral greatness and worthiness being attributed to the faults of the great – that is, to evil. Has La Rochefoucauld given us something more profound than a flippant, punning quip? I think he has. Through the ironies that sparkle in the word "great," he offers us a warning against the influence of such powerful figures. And so crisp a maxim does not fade away.

The eighteenth-century English scholar and critic, Dr Johnson, was, unlike Pascal and La Rochefoucauld, disinclined to reduce a complex moral dilemma to a cryptic maxim and move on. In his *Rambler* essay on "The Modern Novel" (1750), Johnson states the dilemma clearly and then inserts a severe "but" that cuts in the opposite direction from Pascal's "but":

> There have been men indeed splendidly wicked, whose endowments threw a brightness on their crimes, and whom scarce any villainy made perfectly detestable, because they could never be wholly divested of their excellences; but such have been in all ages the great corrupters of the world, and their resemblance ought no more be preserved, than the art of murdering without pain.... Vice, for vice is necessary to be shown, should always disgust; nor should the graces of gaiety, or the dignity of courage, be so united with it, as to reconcile it to the mind.[4]

Johnson believes so strongly in the persuasiveness of literature that he disapproves of assigning sympathetic traits to immoral characters. This principle becomes the basis for his first criticism of Shakespeare: that the dramatist is more concerned to please us than to instruct us. I find Johnson's aversion to villains of mixed and divided temperament naive and obtuse, if only for reasons of verisimilitude. We continue to expect that a novel be true to life in some essential way. But Johnson was dead right in insisting – as did Plato and Rousseau – that what we read, see, and hear as entertainment has strong effects on us, not just on our feelings and imagination but also on our behavior. It would be nearly a century before a fully articulated art for art's sake doctrine came on the scene to separate art from life. It would be more than two centuries before a free-market publisher and pornographer, Larry Flynt, would be heroized in a movie as a champion of free speech, would be invited to university debates, and would state without challenge, "I think adults can read anything they want without being corrupted."[5] Dr Johnson's understanding of human nature reaches deeper than Larry Flynt's.

Before proceeding to further stories to test our mettle, I should like to propose a few distinctions among different forms of evil, distinctions that emerge in part from what I have said so far. I see four categories.

Natural evil occurs in the form of elemental disasters and scourges, which may affect any of us and over which we have limited control. In the years immediately following the Lisbon Earthquake of 1755, the intellectual and theological debate over the meaning of that event contributed to the questioning of the Christian faith.

Moral evil refers to actions undertaken to harm or exploit others in contravention of accepted moral principles or statutes within a society. These actions are subject to judgement and punishment, mitigation and aggravation, repentance and remission. In societies shaped by Western traditions, Greco-Roman law and Judeo-Christian ideals merge in a gradually changing heritage that defines morality.

Radical evil applies to immoral behavior so pervasive in a person or a society that moral scruples and constraints have been utterly abandoned. The ethos of the Marquis de Sade, of the Soviet Gulag, and of the Nazi Holocaust belong to this form of evil so extreme that it can no longer recognize its own atrocity. Lenin stated it forcefully: "The dictatorship means – learn this once and for all – unrestrained power based on force, not on law."[6]

Metaphysical evil designates an assenting and approving attitude toward moral and radical evil, as evidence of superior will and power in human beings. Thus, forms of evil arising from human agency are given a status as inevitable, effectively a reversion to natural evil in the first category. And thus, the cruelest monsters and tyrants become normalized in the perspective of history and of "the survival of the fittest" in evolution. Metaphysical evil nullifies all attempts to establish constraints of law and social compact. Pascal was peering all too uncritically in this direction. La Rochefoucauld cautioned us subtly against this form of evil. The twentieth century has conferred astonishingly widespread respect on the attitude of metaphysical evil by honoring the thought of Nietzsche.

Such definitions and distinctions clear the air and supply us with principles and nuances to argue about. In thinking and teaching, we cannot go far without them. I continue, however, to find equal revelation about evil in narratives. Stories supply specific details about character, about setting, and about the passage of time, which are the essentials of our moral existence. When a number of different cultures concur in identifying an author as having profound insights into a particular aspect of life, then I believe we have good reason to read that author with attention. On the subject of evil, one author has earned prominence that has few close rivals. In many of his writings, Dostoevsky presents different versions of a single situation: the failed attempt by an individual or a group of individuals to extend the moral evil of their actions into the purer and more intense domain of radical evil. Even *Notes from Underground*, behind its compulsive comedy and satire, sketches a weak version of this situation. *The Demons* and *Crime and Punishment*, in comparison, develop a strong version that overrides elements of comedy and satire. Dostoevsky's major works deal primarily with forms of evil and fanaticism released by "new ideas." In this respect, Dostoevsky remains astonishingly timely. For a teacher of literature, his work occupies an essential place in the curriculum. A character like Raskolnikov anticipates the essence and allure of Nietzsche's thought. Dostoevsky also provides, in Raskolnikov's friend Razumikhin and in the police inspector Porfiry, a mature rejoinder, both spoken and lived, to these destructive new ideas.

I wish now to pose an odd question about a Russian author of the following generation, who grew up in much the same society as Dostoevsky and who, through his practice as a physician and his professional familiarity with prisons, knew as much about the underside of life as Dostoevsky. Why don't we turn to Chekhov to inform ourselves about the compulsions and evasions of evil as we do to Dostoevsky? Chekhov's plays and stories contain despair to the point of suicide, pointless and fatal duels, perfidy and deception in endless variations. Chekhov is essentially more of a realist than Dostoevsky, much of whose force lies in a strong proclivity to melodrama, caricature, and hallucinatory scenes. In an 1887 letter to his landlady, M. V. Kiseleva, Chekhov defends a story called "Mire" about how a grasping provincial courtesan half corrupts two intelligent and respectable cousins, who cannot resist her charms. Literature must be able to portray all of life including "the dunghill," Chekhov insists, even though the depiction of evil affects readers in very different ways. Echoing the French critic Taine, he states, "A writer should be as objective as a chemist." Yet Chekhov has written this stout defense of literary freedom with reference to a singularly innocent story. In "Mire," the two matched protagonists may misbehave a bit, but their embarrassed laughter at their own behavior is an appropriate response to their social situation. "Mire" provides almost too strong a title for a story in which any evil emerges briefly from the milieu and is absorbed back into it. Even the stunningly self-reliant woman, who impresses both men with her beauty and talents, seems more a challenge to stuffiness than a sinister and corrupting influence.

"Mire," like most of Chekhov's stories and plays, is a work without a villain. He depicts everything, dunghills and all. Yet the self-deprecating, tentative actions of his characters leave the impression that, in their weakness, they exist as the victims of natural evil. Awful things happen, but no one must assume full moral responsibility for them. Even Natasha, the most self-absorbed and unfeeling character in *Three Sisters*, does not fill the role of a moral agent driving the action, like Stavrogin in *The Devils*. Chekhov deals with evil, but he pushes it constantly in the opposite direction from that of Dostoevsky. Chekhov moves it through prolonged silences and inappropriate laughter toward natural evil about which we can do very little. Dostoevsky moves evil with prolonged intellectual discussions and growing horror toward radical evil and its self-justification in metaphysical evil. As a result, Chekhov is consoling to read; Dostoevsky disturbing. They make a more contrasting and revealing pair of opposites than Tolstoy and Dostoevsky.

Seventy-five years ago a homicide shocked the nation: Nathan Leopold (age 20) and Richard Loeb (age 19), two precocious college graduates in Chicago, each from a wealthy family, kidnapped and murdered a fourteen-year-old boy from their neighborhood. Then they tried to extort a ransom from the boy's family. As the result of some remarkable police work, their bumbling soon betrayed them, and they confessed.

The two youths were neither deprived not mistreated. They could look forward to a brilliant future. Why this seemingly senseless crime? They sought the thrill, the kind of elation Baudelaire imagined in a momentary experience. But they planned this empty crime over a long period of time. They hoped it would demonstrate that they could conceive and carry out a perfect crime. They sought a physical and sexual bond by sharing the responsibility for such an inhuman action – a dimension not covered by the court proceedings. And such a crime would demonstrate their superiority to and exemption from the ordinary laws of mankind. After their confessions, Leopold enthusiastically expounded Nietzsche's superman philosophy to attentive reporters.

The young men's defense was conducted by Clarence Darrow, the most celebrated trial lawyer of the era. He had them plead guilty without plea bargaining. That way they would appear before a single judge to decide the sentence. The hearing, with many witnesses for both sides, lasted more than a month. Having avoided the unwanted jury trial by guilty pleas that acknowledged the sanity of his clients, Darrow deployed witnesses and arguments to prove that the defendants were "mentally impaired." One of the psychologists testifying stated that Leopold and Loeb formed a rare combination of personalities that produced a *folie à deux*. In his magisterial summation, published in newspapers nationwide, Darrow cited the Nietzsche influence at some length. He turned it into a mitigating circumstance. Of Loeb, the more intellectual of the two: "Your Honor, it is hardly fair to hang a nineteen-year-old boy for the philosophy that was taught him at the university." Of Leopold: the fact that he lived and practiced the superman myth was evidence of a "diseased mind."

The most persuasive and finally successful part of Darrow's argument was a plea against the inhumanity of capital punishment as no improvement over the talion law of an eye for an eye. As usual, he quoted copiously from A. E. Housman and Omar Khayyam. The judge sentenced Leopold and Loeb to life plus ninety-nine years. But along the way Darrow had stretched and even exceeded legal limits in his efforts to transform guilt or conscious evil into insanity. The prosecutor, Crowe, argued back tellingly in his summation. He quoted Theodore Roosevelt's response to a plea of insanity by a death-row prisoner:

> I have scant sympathy with a plea of insanity advanced to save a man's life from the consequences of his crime, when, unless that crime had been committed, it would have been impossible to persuade any reasonable authority to place him in an insane asylum.

No friend or familiar had ever considered Leopold or Loeb mentally incompetent before their crime. And Crowe felt compelled to reveal Darrow's deepest convictions about the nature of crime. Crowe read to the packed court and into the historic record a statement that Darrow had made twenty years earlier to prisoners in the Cook County Jail in Chicago:

> The reason I talk to you on the question of crime, its cause and cure, is because I really do not believe the least in crime. There is no such thing as a crime, as the word is generally understood. I do not believe that there is any sort of distinction between the moral condition in and out of jail. One is just as good as the other. The people here can no more help being here than the people outside can avoid being outside. I do not believe that people are in jail because they deserve to be.

It sounded for a time as if Darrow were being put on trial. First, he partly excused the boys' evil actions by attributing them to the influence of Nietzsche's ideas, the ideas of a man who went mad. Second, Darrow had publicly advocated ideas about social determinism and the non-existence of crime and moral responsibility. These ideas, if accepted, would not merely mitigate the crime; they would undermine the entire judicial system in which he was participating as a major player and would eliminate from social relations any guiding principles of good and evil, sanity and madness, innocence and crime. This disturbing revelation close to the end of the trial did not halt Darrow's juggernaut against capital punishment. But it demonstrated that highly articulate and influential persons close to the criminal justice system may entertain notions about the nature of evil and free will utterly at odds with the basic principles of that system. The Leopold and Loeb case has not lost its savor.

The last story I want to examine is neither a literary work nor a court case. The movie *Pulp Fiction* (1994) represents several murderous episodes in gory detail, sets all the action in a criminal milieu where such acts are considered normal and justified (with the exception of one awkward accident), and surrounds the incidents with small talk and compulsive wise-cracking. After you have adjusted to the thick layer of obscenities, one frequent four-letter word begins to designate the character trait held up by the film for admiration: that word is *cool*. Mr Wolf, the chief mobster's troubleshooter, efficiently and unflappably directs the cleanup of everyone's bloody mess and restores the normal order of crime. Mr Wolf provides the nearest approach to a moral center in the story. He is supremely cool.

One brief scene, in which a character chooses the most cruel available weapon with which to avenge himself, unmistakably satirizes the conventions of splatter films. One after another he picks up and then rejects for the next candidate a hammer, a baseball bat, and a chain-saw, settling finally and triumphantly on a samurai sword. This is vaudeville. Is it possible that Tarantino intends to mock the film industry's crass exploitation of criminal violence? Some viewers and critics believe he does. But the sequences of the movie as shot and edited display themselves as complicit with the criminal violence they depict. Except for the weapon scene just mentioned, nothing suggests that this film sees around or beyond the horrible actions it portrays with the utmost cool. They just happen, without revulsion, without greatness. By depicting evil in this fashion, the film neutralizes it, absorbs it into ordinary life broken by a few thrills and laughs, and desensitizes us to evil.

After I had presented a similar analysis of *Pulp Fiction* in a lecture on Swift and satire, a few of my male students defended the movie vehemently as satire. They maintained that it sensitizes the audience to violence and crime. We did not persuade one another. I continue to find, after later viewings, that *Pulp Fiction* mitigates the behavior it represents, as Darrow tried to mitigate the evil deeds of Leopold and Loeb even after legally conceding their guilt. But in one respect *Pulp Fiction* carries us further than Darrow away from responsibility and guilt. In the ideal of "cool" complicity in criminal violence lurks the suggestion, spotted by Pascal and La Rochefoucauld, of greatness *in* evil and *of* evil. Plausibly, a form of greatness can be found in a few tragic roles, like that of Aeschylus' Orestes, in whom lucidity and true remorse finally expunge the evil of matricide. Then, however, it is no longer greatness *in* and *of* evil, but greatness in *overcoming* evil and attaining wisdom. The "cool" of *Pulp Fiction*, in contrast, transports us first into the pervasiveness of radical evil and then back to Rameau's Nephew's metaphysical evil – his approbation of the Renegade of Avignon. Evil is not overcome; evil is accepted and admired.

I close with a troubling quotation from Emerson. Toward the end of "Experience," one of his most skeptical and disillusioned essays, Emerson writes the remarkable passage on evil from which I drew my epigraph: "We believe in ourselves, as we do not believe in others. We permit all things to ourselves, and that which we call sin in others, is experiment for us."[7]

The term "experiment," cousin to "experience," links Emerson's thoughts to Ethan Brand's search for the Unpardonable Sin and to Baudelaire's bohemian indulging his perverse cruelty. And Emerson's transformation of objective sin into subjective "experiment" suggests a method of discovering greatness in evil, as imagined by Pascal and La Rochefoucauld. In this strongly observant passage, Emerson appears to take no stand, to observe from afar. Then, a dozen lines later, he produces a sentence that casts light on every case and story I have cited: "For there is no crime in intellect." I read that sentence as deeply cautionary to our era. Our culture, and in particular the institution of the university, has contrived over the past few decades to transform sin and evil into a positive term: *transgression*. As used by postmodern critics today, transgression refers to conduct that aspires to Emerson's moral experiment and to an implied form of greatness in evil.

Let us beware of applying our intellects to condoning evil and even to making ourselves into "splendidly wicked people." After the century that has twice spawned massive state terrorism, in Soviet communism and in Nazi fascism, we cannot afford such blindness to history and such moral naiveté.

Notes

1 The closest approximation can be found in his final long poem, "Le Voyage," about death as the only remaining novelty: "Partir pour partir." ["Leave for the sake of leaving."]

2 Translation by Roger Shattuck. In French: B. Pascal, *Pensées*, L. Lafuma (ed.), New York, Dutton, 1960, number 526.

3 Translation by Roger Shattuck. Pascal, *Pensées*, Lafuma (ed.), numbers 200 and 756.

4 S. Johnson, "The Modern Novel," *The Rambler*, no. 4, Saturday, March 31, 1750, pp. 24, 26.

5 Quoted in "Preacher and Pornographer Rehash Supreme Court Case," *Inside UVA*, November 7, 1997, p. 5.

6 Quoted by D. M. Thomas in *Alexander Solzhenitsyn: A Century in His Life*, New York, St Martin's Press, 1998, p. 13.

7 R. W. Emerson, *The Collected Works of Ralph Waldo Emerson*, vol. III, *Essays: Second Series*, J. Slater (ed.), Cambridge, MA, The Belknap Press of Harvard University Press, p. 45.

4 The Plot of Suffering

AIDS and Evil

David B. Morris

> About suffering, they were never wrong,
> The old masters, how well they understood
> Its human position . . .
>   W. H. Auden, "Musée des Beaux Arts"

"Our continued existence as gay men upon the face of this earth is at stake," wrote playwright and novelist Larry Kramer in 1983; "unless we fight for our lives, we shall all die."[1] His angry, alarmist outcry occurred at the moment when the number of known victims killed by a mysterious new disease had recently climbed over one thousand. In the two years prior to 1983, widely scattered news reports and medical bulletins had referred to a shadowy fatal ailment called GRID, Gay Related Immune Deficiency, so-called because most of its victims were male homosexuals. Why were they dying? Nobody knew, although wild theories, paranoia, and outright anti-gay bigotry began to circulate almost at once. (With graveyard humor, New York City hospital staff invented their own acronym for the disease: WOGS, or Wrath of God Syndrome.) Only in mid-1984 did scientists isolate the cause of AIDS in a retrovirus – labeled HTLV-Three by Americans, LAV by the French, and ultimately HIV (human immunodeficiency virus). Two years later, the US Public Health Service estimated that between 1 and 1.5 million Americans were infected with HIV. In 1991 the World Health Organization concluded that the number of people HIV-positive by the year 2000 would stand at some 40 million worldwide – but the estimates kept going up.[2] What the popular media first described as a "gay plague" has grown into a global pandemic that threatens people of all ages and genders – even newborn infants. The gay community has been hit especially hard. "Because fate had placed me on the front line of this epidemic from the very beginning," Kramer explained the role (part Jeremiah, part foot soldier) that he felt thrust upon him, "I was a witness to much history that other writers were not."[3]

There is no doubt that AIDS has reshaped the postmodern era. The fear and suspicion that it introduced into human sexual relations have, as philosopher Jacques Derrida observes, "irreversibly affected our experience of desire."[4] Fortunately, the prognosis of imminent holocaust is not so grim as when Kramer issued his 1983 alarm to the gay community. Advances in pharmacology are beginning to transform AIDS – at least in the developed world – into a manageable, if still deadly, chronic illness. Throughout central and east Africa, however, and elsewhere across the developing world, death from wasting symptoms of the so-called "thin disease" is swift and sure. Even where treatment is affordable, AIDS continues to destroy lives, families, and communities. A new popular literature has emerged – including film and television – that chronicles how AIDS has turned parent against child, straight against gay, employer against employee, lover against lover.[5] AIDS also still carries the stigma attached to high-risk groups such as homosexuals, intravenous drug-users, and prostitutes. As a sexually transmitted fatal disease, it evokes the emotional charge always latent in the volatile bond between death and eroticism, so that real effort is required to see AIDS patients merely as people who are ill. Patients, when not tacitly or openly blamed for their illness, are too often viewed as helpless victims caught in the grip of a hideous creature. The science-based Public Television series *Nova* employed exactly this horror-film scenario to provide the structure for a widely shown documentary on AIDS, in which doctors and scientists were cast as heroic dragon-slayers.[6] The person who falls ill with AIDS today falls inescapably into this net of tacit meanings and subliminal narratives.

No contemporary affliction illustrates better than AIDS how the biology of human illness intersects with cultural practices that increasingly reshape it. In effect, while the human immunodeficiency virus was silently digging into the genetic materials of the billions of cells it attacked across the globe, activists with the passion of Larry Kramer (including his critics within the gay community) were generating a discourse of protest, analysis, argument, fear, elegy, and denunciation unprecedented in recent medical history. AIDS-talk, from scientists to TV hosts, encircled the virus in meaning, with widely varying results.[7] It helped some patients and activists to work out a new sense of their own identity, while for others the babble of conflicting voices threatened to undermine a stable sense of self. Public-health posters and (to a lesser degree) televised ads reinforced the discourse with images of healthy, beautiful, erotic bodies threatened or poisoned by AIDS.[8] As Paula A. Treichler has shown in a series of essays, the biology of HIV infection cannot be cleanly disentangled from this ongoing cultural construction of AIDS.[9] Anyone who suffers from AIDS in the developed world suffers within a culture where their illness has been saturated with multiple meanings, ambiguous information, and a conflict of competing discourses. Such suffering, as we will see, bears the distinctive imprint of postmodern transformations.

The Transformation of Evil

Evil, like suffering, has been transformed by postmodern culture. It doubtless constitutes a truism of contemporary thought that evil has shared in the same loss of credulity suffered by the comprehensive explanatory systems or – as Jean-François Lyotard famously calls them – "meta-narratives" that formerly explained or contained it.[10] This truism is surely accurate, if incomplete. Paul Ricoeur in *The Encyclopedia of Religion*, summarizing and extending his earlier work, describes four dominant myths worldwide that have addressed the origin of evil: chaos myths, myths of an evil god, myths of the exiled soul, and myths of a lost paradise.[11] Myths of origin fall among the metanarratives that come under suspicion in post-modern thought, but in Western cultures the most powerful and still inter-mittently persistent myth describing the origin of evil is doubtless the vision of a lost paradise.

John Milton's epic *Paradise Lost* gave influential expression to the long-standing view that evil is an omnipresent threat and central event in human history. The threat of evil is felt as so powerful that Milton writes in effect within the formal tradition of theodicies that explicitly set out to justify God's ways to man, especially in creating or permitting evil. Milton depicts human history, in contrast to the timeless innocence of Eden, as beginning with the temptation scene and the triumph of evil, when Eve disobeys God and succumbs to the wiles of Satan. William Blake's illustration of the scene is faithful to the spirit of Milton's text in depicting Adam, at the fateful moment, looking away from Eve, with back turned. Adam's back-turned posture carries a crucial moral meaning: he simply cannot see or will not attend to the presence of evil, as embodied in the well-spoken serpent.

Attention is an important ethical state for Milton, more significant at times than heroic action. They too serve God, he says in the sonnet on his blindness, who only stand and wait, attentively. The flowery garland that Adam has been weaving for Eve – now fallen beside his left foot – is more than a sign of love or perhaps, for Milton, even of uxorious folly: it is a prophecy of their own impending fall. It locates the triumph of evil in the failed attention that ignores the dangers – from within and without – that continuously surround us. Human history, for Milton, is life lived, un-cloistered, in the heat and dust of constant temptation and in the all too easily ignored presence of evil.

Evil in the West has never regained the prominence, theological and dramatic, that it achieved in *Paradise Lost*. Little more than half a century later, at the dawn of the Industrial Revolution, its central position had been subtly but thoroughly eroded. *An Essay on Man* by Alexander Pope announces its ambition to rival Milton in the creation of a theodicy. Pope aims to "vindicate" (not merely "justify," as Milton claimed to do) the ways of God to humankind. Pope's lengthy vindication of divine goodness in four verse epistles, however, manages with only two appearances of the word "evil." His preferred term to describe catastrophes and wrongdoing is not evil but the milder, evasive term "ills." In effect, while Milton struggles with the problem of evil, including the omnipresent threat, dire consequences, and deep mystery that evil represents, Pope worries about the appearance of evil. Evil for Pope is not a cosmic force continuously at war with humankind, daily tempting the soul and threatening to plunge us into everlasting fire, but rather a cognitive illusion: what we misinterpret as evil is, if understood rightly, a component of "universal good." True, Pope retains a trace of the older vocabulary of evil when he employs a distinction between "physical or moral ill" common in theological accounts. If the distinction remains, however, its force is lost in the light of a rational theology that has no room for mysteries so potent that they once demanded nothing less than a mythic imagination. Now evil (under a new name) can be handled in a single line as the effect of errant will and natural change. Evil in its traditional Satanic presence is simply irrelevant to Pope's description of Colley Cibber or the Walpole administration, much as we do not need evil in order to account for the flooding of the Mississippi River or the misdeeds of Richard Nixon.

The decline of Satan is one measure of the erosion suffered by evil in the modern world. In George Cruickshank's lithograph "Introduction to the Gout" (1818), evil has dwindled to the machinations of a comic demon, decently clad to observe pre-Victorian etiquette. The parodic status of evil here serves to mark the vast distance separating modern audiences from Miltonic traditions of hellfire, torment, and moral vigilance.

For Cruickshank, the pain of gout has its origin not in theological traditions of evil but in the luxurious lifestyles of the aristocracy and idle rich. Like Pope, Cruickshank sees no deep mythos at work, no Job-like enigma at the heart of disaster and suffering. An exploding volcano – an occasion for earlier meditations on sin and divine wrath, which even Pope still needed to confront under the old vocabulary of physical evil – is now merely an object of sublime art suitable for a wealthy collector. Culture, embodied in the overfed, upper-class, tasteless epicure, tells us everything we need to know about pain that once seemed the genuine signature of evil.

The postmodern world – despite our skepticism about grand narratives and our erosion of trust in mythic accounts – has not witnessed the absolute disappearance of evil, nor has Satan wholly died. In its notorious eclecticism, postmodernism retains elements from the past, which are of course deracinated and transformed in their new context, like an ancient Greek portico stuck onto a skyscraper. Televangelists regularly thunder against sin and evil in their fund-raising ministries. The so-called death of Satan becomes the occasion for an academic critique of liberal failures to understand the reality of evil and to give it a needed place in our civic and moral imagination.[12] Less tendentiously, a few theologians, historians, feminists, and philosophers continue to study the perennial issues associated with evil and to offer insightful analysis.[13] It is even possible to find talented people from various walks of life brought together in 1987 at a Texas symposium to discuss the contemporary fate of evil. (In proper media-centered, postmodern style, portions of the discussion reappeared in a televised Bill Moyers PBS special entitled "Facing Evil."[14]) The fact is that evil in the postmodern era – even as a topic of conversation – has not so much disappeared as taken on the changed shapes of a period in which theological and mythic accounts of a lost paradise no longer ring true.

Indeed, the twentieth century has witnessed catastrophes (from world war to genocide) so immense and so chilling as to demand and, on occasion, to receive serious discussion, such as Hannah Arendt's influential treatment of Adolph Eichmann and the banality of evil.[15] Arendt's view of Eichmann is especially helpful in suggesting that evil has not disappeared but rather taken on distinctive new shapes. It seems clear that she detects a modernist transformation of evil in the Nazi employment of such invisibly omnipresent inventions as the assembly line, mass transit, and the bureaucratic routine. The decades that have passed since the close of the Second World War and the advent of postmodern times have seen evil not so much transformed as turned inside out. Evil has been long understood by theologians and by popular audiences (even Cruickshank invokes it) as the *cause* of suffering.[16] The postmodern era has redefined suffering *as* evil. Suffering becomes one of the few agreed-upon new shapes that evil assumes in the postmodern world.

The postmodern reformulation of the bond between suffering and evil finds examples not only throughout popular culture, where prolonged suffering is construed as the worst thing that can befall someone, but also, surprisingly, in the sciences and social sciences. Timothy Anders, for example, is unusual mainly in employing the postmodern tools of evolutionary psychology to argue that "the ultimate source of all evil is the biological capacity for suffering."[17] Here again we see the traditional relation between evil and suffering turned inside out: evil is no longer the source of suffering, but rather suffering is the source of evil. French-Jewish philosopher Emmanuel Levinas provides an especially thought-provoking account of this reversal in his essay "Useless Suffering." Levinas writes self-consciously from a late twentieth-century stance in which our awareness of massive cruelty and of unprecedented suffering exceeds any possible justification in the language of traditional theology. "This is the century," he reminds us, "that in thirty years has known two world wars, the totalitarianisms of right and left, Hitlerism and Stalinism, Hiroshima, the Gulag, and the genocides of Auschwitz and Cambodia."[18] The millions of victims crushed in all this torture and destruction cannot for Levinas be encompassed within traditional religious perspectives which understand evil through its relation to God's will. In this new context, which he believes requires a radical rethinking of evil, Levinas seeks the basis for what he calls a faith without theodicy. "All evil," he asserts starkly, "refers to suffering."[19]

Suffering, in Levinas's account, takes on the quality of evil from its combination of destructive pain coupled with absolute and intrinsic uselessness. Suffering, for the person who suffers, is in his view wholly without meaning. It is simply the experience of an overwhelming, violent, and cruel negation – "extreme passivity, impotence, abandonment and solitude"[20] – in which every human effort to affirm coherence or value drains away into absurdity. It is, Levinas writes, the "*impasse* of life and being."[21] Such impasse for Levinas finds its archetype in the Holocaust of the Jews under Hitler: "the paradigm of gratuitous human suffering, where evil appears in its diabolical horror."[22] Within the darkness of such diabolical evil redefined as an extreme and useless suffering, within the horror of utter meaningless-ness and of crushing impersonal force, however, Levinas also finds the hope for a saving transformation. The source of this transformation lies in what he calls "the inter-human order."

The "inter-human order" for Levinas signifies not merely the everyday political or social worlds but the ethical position of the self (prior to all practical politics or implied social contracts) as inescapably bound up with others. From this ethical perspective based upon a recognition of the Other, the suffering of another person – while absolutely useless, meaningless, and inexorably evil to the person who suffers – can take on a meaning through the "inter-human" claim it makes upon us as witnesses: it solicits and calls us, invoking the recourse that people have always recognized to help one another. Further, where such solicitation finds an answering response, absolute and meaningless suffering does not lose its quality of evil for the sufferer but instead becomes transformed, in the self who responds, into what Levinas calls a meaningful suffering for the suffering of someone else. This difficult reciprocity within suffering makes sense in the context of Levinas's distinctive style of postmodern thought, where an ethics of the inter-human is not an obligation derived from higher principles but rather the principle from which philosophy and ethics must begin. The importance of Levinas here lies not only in his identification of evil with suffering but also in his demonstration that postmodern suffering – cut free from traditional theodicies – clearly differs from suffering as it was understood at least from the time of Milton through the modernist era.

Suffering: Modern and Postmodern

Postmodern thought differs from modernist thinking not only in the creation of an absolute identity between evil and suffering but also in the develop-ment of a new idea of suffering. The famous poem "Musée des Beaux Arts" by W. H. Auden offers a strong example of the modernist view that is rejected or revised in postmodern versions of suffering. Auden's poem – based upon the famous painting *Landscape with the Fall of Icarus* (1555), by Pieter Brueghel the Elder – depicts suffering as a quintessentially individual, private, and solitary experience. This modernist view construes the act of suffering, even though embedded in a rich social context, as occurring in an almost impenetrable solitude, like Icarus falling into the sea as the workaday world goes about its business, with only his lower legs visible in the extreme right corner of Brueghel's canvas.

As Auden depicts it, such impenetrable solitude is almost built into the structure of suffering. The problem is not that we turn away from evil and disaster, Adam-like, as if unable to foresee or to bear it, or as if deliberately refusing to assist. While suffering regularly disturbs and threatens us, Auden does not represent the turning away from suffering as moral failure, a lapse, say, of foresight, charity, or courage. He depicts aversion or detachment, instead, as the outcome of a structural position we cannot help but occupy. Suffering occurs in a social world where non-sufferers always find their own lives more absorbing and immediate, where nature and commerce continue in their appointed course oblivious to individual disaster. The plowman never looks up; the expensive ship sails on. If suffering should fall unavoidably within our field of vision, Auden insists that we cannot escape our built-in position of detachment. Not even the Old Masters, he suggests, could somehow place us in direct relation to another person's suffering. Their triumph – straining the limits of art – lies in forcing us to recognize and to contemplate our fated detachment as each of us, like Icarus, suffers alone.

The significance of Auden's poem lies in the clarity with which it presents the modernist myth (a myth it represents as uncontestable truth) that suffering is an individual, private, and solitary state of inwardness. From a postmodern perspective, it seems clear that Auden invokes Brueghel and the Old Masters in effect to universalize and confirm what is a historically and culturally specific modernist interpretation of suffering, as recognizably modernist as the gaunt, skeletal, solitary human figures sculpted by Alberto Giacometti. As heirs of modernism, of course, we respond to a persuasiveness in Auden's view that the normal human "position" in relation to suffering mandates a glasslike separation and detachment. Yet, this modernist myth concerning the inwardness and isolation of suffering is not necessarily confirmed by Brueghel's painting. It is uncertain, in fact, whether Brueghel's painting deals with suffering at all. The painting could equally depict violent death or the consequences of over-reaching. Even if we grant that the painting deals with suffering, Brueghel's luminous depiction of everyday life – the shining furrows, dazzling sea, and dreamlike city – might suggest that suffering lies wholly outside the realm of daily experience: it is not so much private and inward as utterly alien: we cannot grasp it any more than we can make sense of a demigod falling from the sky. Auden's reading of Brueghel is powerful precisely because it seems to validate as universal what is at last merely a limited and historical modernist interpretation of suffering. From a postmodern perspective, suffering is never wholly individual, private, inward, and solitary, despite our inability to inhabit another human consciousness. Postmodern suffering, as we will see, contains important public and social – or inter-human – dimensions.

The postmodern interpretation of suffering as necessarily public and social stands in vivid contrast to the modernist emphasis on isolation and silence. The silence attributed to suffering in modernist views is almost a cliché: a corollary of the argument that suffering is private, inward, and unknowable. There are obviously no words to convey an experience construed as so inaccessible to others that it lies beyond language. The cliché of silent suffering, however, while it recognizes real limitations of speech and knowledge, must somehow be reconciled with an equally obvious and proliferating discourse of lament, elegy, litigation, and victim-mongering. Postmodern suffering not only seeks a voice but also, however imperfectly, enters vigorously into the public discourses and speech genres of specific communities. A postmodern approach thus recognizes that suffering in some sense follows the contours of various established discourses, much as an academic analysis like this one will follow the conventions of scholarly discourse, including footnotes, reference to contemporary thinkers, and correct grammar. Methodist hymns, by contrast, treat human suffering within a speech genre where none of the social patterns that govern scholarly essays apply – or even make sense. Suffering, from a postmodern perspective, cannot be disentangled from the linguistic and narrative turns that so deeply color contemporary knowledge. Postmodern suffering belongs inside – inextricably connected with and shaped by – the public, social domain of story and language.

The specific question at issue here is quite basic. Why does it matter for people with AIDS and for an understanding of evil that postmodernism asks us to recognize how every voice is shaped and constrained by the speech genres of a specific social community at a particular historical moment? It matters because the public discourses of distinct historical communities also shape and constrain how we talk about suffering, how we talk when suffering, and, ultimately, how we suffer.

The major change that typifies postmodern versions of suffering and of evil can be identified in the concept of social suffering. "Social suffering," as Arthur Kleinman, Veena Das, and Margaret Lock contend, "results from what political, economic, and institutional power does to people and, reciprocally, from how these forms of power themselves influence responses to social problems."[23] Contributors to the book-length volume *Social Suffering* discuss the forms of affliction that characterize such political, economic, and institutional applications of power as the rape of women in India during the struggle for independence from Britain, the imposition of Maoism in China, and, inevitably, the Holocaust. Moreover, the writings of Michel Foucault have shown how social power works not only through traditional top-down political, economic, and institutional hierarchies but also through widely distributed informal networks of professional knowledge and cultural discourse. Suffering, when viewed in this postmodern perspective, is never strictly private, inward, and individual. It is trans-personal, discursive, or, as Levinas says, inter-human. Its sources lie not in some unknowable or ungraspable fatality – like the will of the gods or the operations of a mysterious curse – but rather in social structures and in cultural practices. Individuals suffer only within the context of far larger social forces and actions that give their suffering its distinctive historical shapes. One way to think about this postmodern conception of evil as social suffering is to imagine a shift from myth to plot.

Myths deal with archetypal patterns or large abstract structures of experience that always exceed the dimensions of a single culture or society. In discussing myths of evil, Paul Ricoeur emphasizes how myth "incorporates our fragmentary experience of evil within great narratives of origin."[24] The postmodern skepticism concerning grand narratives carries over into a skepticism concerning myths of evil. Myth and plot clearly overlap, of course, in the sense that every myth tells a story, but plot introduces us to a more detailed and prosaic level of narrative. It moves us from timelessness to time. Plot gives us heroes or heroines who are not the thousand-faced figures of myth but distinctive people with local addresses: Quixote, Crusoe, Pip, Mrs Dalloway, Joseph K. Plots, too, tend to focus on a specific, concrete, and unique sequence of actions. They describe a world in which this unique sequence of actions and choices, not an underlying mythic pattern, is what determines individual destinies. Plot, moreover, invites a detailed analysis of causation. It gives wider play than myth to the operations of chance and contingency, while also allowing readers or spectators to acknowledge elements of narrative structure, such as the recognition scene or turning point, that distinguish causal sequences from mere happenstance or fate. Plot, in short, immerses us in a world where suffering and evil emerge as distinct from the universal forces represented in myth. It allows us to understand evil and suffering as, no matter how deeply imbued with ineradicable traces of mystery, at least in part the outcome of specific inter-human actions and distinctive social arrangements.

These heuristic differences between myth and plot – evoked as a framework for analysis of suffering and evil in the postmodern age – find a clear illustration in the work of Gustavo Gutiérrez.[25] Gutiérrez, known as the founder of Liberation Theology, is a Catholic priest who works in the slums of Lima, Peru. For Gutiérrez, the suffering of the innocent and impoverished masses who inhabit the slums of Lima does not raise traditional theological questions about God's will. He is not concerned with mythic explanations of evil as originating in a lost paradise. For Gutiérrez, we will understand the suffering in the slums of Lima only by identifying the historical oppression of the poor by powerful landowners who receive the support (if not outright blessing) of the Catholic Church. Plot here is not merely an analytical tool that helps clarify the social causes of suffering in the historical actions of wealthy landowners and churchmen. Unlike myth, where the outcome is already foretold, plot has access to the realm of contingency, where human actions may change the outcome of events. Suffering in the slums of Lima, Gutiérrez insists, will not be reversed by medicines or compassion or improved social services, however welcome they might be, but only by the creation of a new and just historical plot that redresses the oppression of the poor. A postmodern vision that understands suffering as inter-human and historical (not solitary, private, inward, and inscrutable) matters for Gutiérrez precisely because it contains an implicit imperative for mobilizing effective social resistance to evil.

AIDS, Suffering, and Plot

AIDS stands prominent among postmodern illnesses. Historian Charles E. Rosenberg articulates the sense in which AIDS is (as he calls it) a distinctively "postmodern epidemic" when he describes the readjustments it requires in traditional thinking. "After a generation of epistemological – and political – questioning of the legitimacy of many disease categories," he writes, "AIDS has exposed the inadequacy of any one-dimensional approach to disease, either the social constructionist or the more conventional mechanistically oriented perspective."[26] AIDS is postmodern especially in requiring an understanding of disease as *both* biological and cultural – biocultural – constituted at the crossroads of biology and culture. An extensive scholarly literature now traces how cultural attitudes and public policies have shaped the course of AIDS as surely as have the workings of the human immunodeficiency virus.[27] Strange as it sounds, while medicine has made progress in devising multiple drug treatments that prolong the life expectancy of AIDS patients, the cultural resources of plot have had an equally serious impact on the lives of people with AIDS. Rosenberg, for example, observes that all epidemics tend to follow the pattern of a drama in four acts, from the initial slow revelation of danger to a "flat and ambiguous" last act. The two middle stages of an epidemic (which he calls "managing randomness" and "negotiating public response") are of course where we stand today with AIDS. Within this larger drama played out as the AIDS epidemic unfolds, there are numerous submerged subjects. Three closely related subplots merit special attention not only for their impact on people suffering from AIDS, but also for their importance in what might be called a cultural struggle to control the AIDS narrative: the plot of origins, the victim plot, and the plot of resistance.

Suffering and evil must come from somewhere. Myths and the grand narratives of origin previously allowed the community to assign both a specific cause and a probable trajectory to its misfortune, even if the cause were as remote and enigmatic as the sin of Adam. In the case of AIDS, one consistent public response – employing the postmodern privilege of importing into the present moment elements from the recent or distant past – was to conflate the contemporary epidemic with earlier notions of plague. The almost automatic recourse to describing AIDS as a plague had consequences that extended far beyond the use of metaphorical language common in everyday speech and in scientific writing. Metaphors are indirect or poetic accounts of origin, and through this metaphorical language AIDS indirectly became entangled with the fragmentary remnants of two myths or grand narratives that have persisted, as if underground, during the postmodern era. It achieved what Susan Sontag calls a "dual metaphoric genealogy": understood both as an invasion and a pollution.[28]

Microbiology soon made it clear how the viral invasion operated at the level of individual cells, often with recourse to the military metaphors that remain a regular feature of contemporary thinking about disease. Yet, the AIDS virus did not operate exactly like other related pathogens, such as the agent responsible for syphilis, where symptoms appear after an incubation of twelve to thirty days. Syphilis was like a visible army whose advance could be mapped and therefore opposed. The exact moment of infection might be determined, in retrospect, and responsibility determined. HIV, however, because it remained dormant within the body, often for many years, operated more like a terrorist: penetrating at a point usually impossible to determine, lurking unseen, then striking in ways impossible to neutralize with a counter-strike, the cause of multiple illnesses that finally wear down the body's immune defense. The problem with the invasion plot is that as yet there is no sure way to defend or to strike back. In addition, it lends itself to a much larger mythic structure in which the virus invades not only individual cells but also entire cultures or countries, much as a plague was always held to originate elsewhere, in some vague or disreputable outside source.

The plot of invasion, then, easily merges with the plot of pollution. AIDS in the West emerged with an unmistakable link to the recently and imperfectly liberated world of gay sex. It was thus linked with a group that was for many years openly oppressed and even despised, whose sexual practices were reviled by various religious leaders and politicians as unnatural, ungodly, and unspeakable. Even prominent members of the gay community, such as Larry Kramer and Randy Shilts, argued that erotic practices associated with the gay bathhouse in its heyday – anonymous coupling, multiple partners, prolific activity, and group sex – were at the very least (in the context of the AIDS epidemic) unhealthy. With the public alarmed at learning that AIDS is an infectious disease, the fear of contagion simply added to latent or open homophobia: gays who contracted AIDS found their suffering enveloped by a poisonous air of stigma and pollution.[29] With the risk of infection unknown, dentists suddenly appeared before their patients wearing masks and rubber gloves. Basketball players injured during play were – through a rule that appeared almost overnight – removed until the bleeding stopped. The heterosexual traffic in one-night stands reportedly dropped off as people in bars worried about infected partners. Everywhere the so-called "gay plague" carried with it the fearful subplot that the straight world too might soon be dragged down into a murky pool of viral pollution and death. Gays with AIDS thus suffered within the context of an accusatory myth as virulent as any fundamentalist rhetoric about divine censure.

Plots of origin associated with past epidemics usually insist that the plague always comes from elsewhere. They permit an afflicted group or nation to imagine that their own pure culture has been contaminated by contact with some foreign site of impurity and deviance. One scenario popular in the mid-1980s had AIDS originating with green monkeys in central Africa, transmitted via infected Africans to Haitians visiting Zaire, then passed to American homosexuals vacationing in Haiti, who brought it back to New York City and passed it on to intravenous drug users.[30] The only story line missing is an absurdist loop in which New York IV drug users conspire to infect an international convention of hemophiliacs. The "green monkey" theory has been fully discredited. Physician Paul F. Farmer has shown how the high incidence of AIDS in Haiti functions to provide a Third-World scapegoat to fulfill First-World needs to affix blame.[31] Despite such demythologizing, however, there is no end to plots of origin, which thrive on the exotic, the unfamiliar, and the remote: some strange locale or marginal group where life is defined by its threatening otherness. While Americans usually locate the origin of AIDS in Africa, one scholar found that a majority of people sampled in Rwanda believed that AIDS came from America.[32] Wherever you are, plague always comes from somewhere else. What makes this plot of revolving origins less than comic is its toxic melodrama of villains and victims. The moral condemnation widely and early affixed to the gay community – as if each case of AIDS originated in some forbidden and polluting sexual act – reveals how a dominant culture composes and rewrites suffering in ways, ultimately, that tend to justify its dominance.

The victim plot is nested within the plots of pollution and invasion, in the sense that dominance requires submission, and submission often requires or generates a victim. AIDS has certainly produced various twists on the plot of victimization. Gays, of course, find themselves often portrayed by the dominant culture in the role of self-victimized victims. They are viewed as responsible for their own suffering because of their sexual orientation and thus are denied the sympathy extended to heterosexuals infected through means such as medical accidents, transfusions of tainted blood, or the follies of a spouse or lover. Americans seem disposed to grant women and children the special status of "innocent" victims – people regarded as either not responsible for their illnesses or inherently weak – but AIDS complicates even this questionable grant of civic immunity. Fearing infection, neighbors banded together to exclude children with AIDS from local schools. Doors slammed shut and families splintered. Mary Fisher, who was infected with AIDS by her husband, reports meeting a beautiful young woman in Harlem, perhaps twenty, who had also contracted AIDS. "I wish I had cancer instead of AIDS," the woman told Fisher. "I could stand the treatments and the pain and my hair falling out. And I'm going to die anyway. But then, at least, my family wouldn't reject me. I could go home."[33]

Women face special hardships. During the years when AIDS was considered almost entirely a gay disease, women's concerns were mostly erased from policy decisions and media accounts. Later, as media and health-care professionals began to acknowledge that women too contracted AIDS, a familiar category appeared alongside the role of innocent victim: woman as prostitute, nymphomaniac, evil parent, and African "other."[34] Here, as in the stigma attached to gay males, culturally scripted plots determined the context within which people with AIDS would not simply suffer but suffer in their appointed role of victims.

Some people with AIDS, male and female, have of course participated in the distinctive postmodern trend that promotes or even celebrates victimhood. The status of victim is among the more sought-after postures in a popular culture where genuine heroes and heroines seem increasingly rare. Today almost everyone with a grievance or injury seems eager to establish his or her claim to be victimized. The sources of this trend are complex and include investigative journalism, zealous attorneys, social service programs, and paranoia in the face of big government, global economic change, and institutional callousness. No doubt many people suffer serious wrongs because of racism, sexism, and a culture of disenfranchisement, in which sense they are indeed victims. What matters most, given the long history of social injustice, is that the public role of victim has suddenly become so attractive. Every television talk show fills its line-up with people eager to discuss the abuse they claim to have suffered. The attraction of public victimhood lies partly in the implicit right it extends to make a claim on others, legal or social. Postmodern suffering, at least as embodied in the self-declared victim, aggressively solicits attention: it refuses to allow the spectator or bystander to turn away. "Look at me," it says. "I am a victim. I have suffered. You owe me." This claim, however, even when well justified, comes with a hidden cost.

In addition to the damage that an embrace of public victimhood may inflict upon people thereby encouraged to view themselves as disabled or dysfunctional, the talk shows simply consume today's victims, exhaust their entertainment value, then seek out tomorrow's fresh sufferers. Suffering, repackaged as entertainment in the postmodern era, finds its most lucrative and popular form in the televised soap opera, a parade of victims, where a commercial version of the Romantic bond between beauty and suffering proves still irresistible. The importance of this complex postmodern trend toward embracing the plot of public victimhood – with its voluble displays of helplessness – lies in the context it creates for understanding the AIDS activists who boldly and deliberately began to rewrite their own suffering as a plot of resistance.

A radically new plot demands a new language. "We condemn attempts to label us as 'victims,' which implies defeat," declares one activist manifesto, "and we are only occasionally 'patients,' which implies passivity, helplessness, and dependence upon the care of others. We are 'people with AIDS.'"[35] AIDSpeak is what this new dialect of resistance came to be called, and it had immediate political consequences in changing the way in which officials discussed public health issues.[36] More important, however, is the resolve of individual AIDS patients to reject the prefabricated role of the suffering victim. As Max Navarre writes from firsthand experience:

> The point is to see AIDS, when it happens to you, less as a defeat and more as an opportunity for creative life management. That might seem glib, but, given the choice between what *The New York Times* recently

called "a shattered life" and seeing AIDS as a chance to live fully on a daily basis, it doesn't take much to realize which view is the more helpful. Taking the bull by the horns is a means of escaping the sentimental soap opera that the media has created around the experience of having AIDS.[37]

Navarre accurately recognizes that televised soap opera constitutes one of the major cultural genres in the West that shape the postmodern experience of suffering. A helpful alternative to the script of "shattered lives" (or what Arthur W. Frank aptly calls "chaos" stories) is not necessarily ready-made.[38] As traditional plots proved confining or oppressive, AIDS activists in many cases had to transform or revalue existing genres into postmodern vehicles of resistance to suffering. Larry Kramer thus turns the open letter into almost a personal art form. Others see a new prominence and purpose in obituaries and memorial services. The NAMES Project AIDS Memorial Quilt transforms a traditional non-narrative American folk art, the quilt, into an immense language-rich and image-rich testimonial composed of more than 40,000 individual three-by-six-foot panels that compose their own fragmentary tales or mini-narratives about the lives stitched into its fabric.[39]

Maybe the most important narrative implicitly contained within the AIDS Memorial Quilt is the unfinished tale of a previously scattered community that (as if for the first time) constitutes and recognizes itself in the experience of shared grief. The new community constituted by the AIDS Memorial Quilt is not restricted to gays or to the families of people with AIDS. The Quilt, in its communal spirit, enfolds everyone who feels moved in its presence and who responds to its implicit assertion that the suffering of people with AIDS must be understood as something other than a traditional narrative of victimhood.

The AIDS Memorial Quilt, however, like much AIDS discourse, rewrites suffering in an elegiac and retrospective mode.[40] By contrast, one especially controversial contribution of Larry Kramer was his role in founding ACT UP (the acronym for "AIDS Coalition to Unleash Power"). The metaphor of unleashed power suggests something violent no longer held under control, while "acting up" adds the ironic connotations of an irrepressible, high-spirited departure from the norms of good behavior. In mobilizing these almost contradictory moods, ACT UP borrowed its most public tactics from the antiwar movement and civil rights movement of the 1960s, with their rediscovery of guerrilla theater. Indeed, the name ACT UP conveys a sense that the theatrical and the unruly have now joined forces. Guerrilla texts authored by the ACT UP collective included chaining themselves to government buildings, throwing vials full of blood-like liquid, and chalking outlines of the dead on city streets. In January 1991 they staged an on-air invasion of the television studio where the CBS Evening News was in progress.[41]

One famous event occurred during services in December 1989 at Saint Patrick's Cathedral in New York City, when ACT UP – joined by the

Women's Health Action Mobilization and other groups – demonstrated against Cardinal John O'Connor, shouting, passing out information, and lying on the floor.[42] The demonstration, beyond mere disruptive tactics, sought to insert a secular text about suffering into a sacred text (the church service) that had seemed to turn its back on AIDS sufferers. Certainly, Cardinal O'Connor had become a symbol of the Catholic church in its intransigent stance concerning homosexuality and AIDS education. The activists, dragged out of the cathedral (while Cardinal O'Connor continued to preach), used their bodies to produce a vivid counter-text: a protest not only against O'Connor and the Church but also, more importantly, against what John M. Clum has called "the victim mentality of many AIDS narratives."[43] Here was a narrative of refusal and resistance: a defiant rejection of elegiac sadness in the face of public and institutional oppression, a posture of action directly opposed to victimization. *Narrative* is an entirely appropriate term to describe this improvisational audio-visual artifact, especially because the ACT UP demonstration received intense media coverage and even prompted a documentary film, *Stop the Church* (1991), directed by Robert Hilferty. O'Connor's parishioners were outraged and dismayed, of course, as intended, but this was not just another nonviolent protest designed to outrage conservatives and to challenge public policy. Sociologist Stanley Aronowitz sees in ACT UP a conscious shift away from the politics of modernism with its belief in the electoral legitimacy of the liberal state. ACT UP, he argues, challenges not the electoral but the *ethical* legitimacy of liberal institutions, institutions such as medicine, health-care agencies, pharmaceutical companies, and even the Church. Its direct, uncompromising challenge to the ethical legitimacy of the liberal state makes ACT UP, in his view, "the quintessential social movement for the era of postmodern politics."[44]

The work of ACT UP illustrates how, from a postmodern perspective, suffering is never strictly an individual, internal, private affair. ACT UP in its practice redefines suffering as social – reconceives it as social suffering – structured in part by the public discourses and institutions that offer us various scripted roles and plots.[45] In its collective protest, ACT UP directly challenges the modernist refrain that suffering is not only radically individual but also essentially unknowable. It has little interest in the qualities of suffering that extend beyond language and culture; the point, for ACT UP, is to mobilize language and culture in the practice of resistance. As its direct action texts imply, culture and language offer not only tools of resistance but also an important approach to whatever is sharable in suffering. They permit us to recognize the implicit narratives that shape and constrain our experience of suffering and to replace genres, plots, and narratives that prove finally inadequate or harmful. At times, such work may reach no further than the small community of activists. Such is the power of narrative and culture, however, that they can also at times serve to extend the boundaries of a moral community, encouraging the wider public to adopt a different view of suffering.[46] Harriet Beecher Stowe provides an especially clear example of this power to reinvent suffering. In fact, *Uncle Tom's Cabin; or Life Among the Lowly* (1852) – the first American novel to sell over a million copies – so strongly engaged popular feeling that Stowe has been cited among the causes of the Civil War. Her sentimental plot of suffering moved contemporary readers not only to weep at the ordeals of a fictional slave but, more important, to acknowledge the experience of slavery *as* suffering and to rearrange the existing social order that had both authorized slavery and denied the suffering it caused.

Suffering, in short, is not a raw datum – a natural phenomenon we can identify and measure – but a social status that we extend or withhold. We extend or withhold it depending largely on whether the sufferer falls within our prevailing narratives of moral community. When an Iraqi truck driver in the Persian Gulf War presumably died in a firestorm of laser-guided missiles, the incident played on American TV as one more proof of superior US technology. (Iraqi soldiers seemed to find Kuwaiti civilians equally disposable.) We do not acknowledge the destruction of people or creatures outside our moral community as suffering, but detach ourselves from their pain as if it were an incomprehensible behavior encountered on some Swiftian island. This is the human position of suffering, not fixed (as Auden implied) but fluid and mobile, set in motion or frozen in place by the cultural narratives we construct. Inside a specific moral community, we employ names like *martyr* and *hero* to inscribe the suffering of our own party within narratives of hallowed sacrifice and epic achievement. The challenge, which AIDS has dramatized so clearly, is to discover postmodern genres and narratives that validate, illuminate, and authenticate suffering while seeking to alleviate and oppose it, resisting narratives that knowingly or unknowingly transform suffering into an occasion for the perpetuation of victimhood.

Evil, from a postmodern perspective, is as malleable as the suffering with which it has increasingly come to be identified. Filmmakers, of course, continue to create stories depicting evil as an indestructible cosmic force, breeding new legions in a distant galaxy, or as a deathless Gothic legacy that lives on in vampires, swamp creatures, and ax murderers. As we might expect, there is no single postmodern voice of evil. Some postmodern voices prove especially gripping because they call upon an archaic and primitive dread that may belong to the evolutionary history of humankind. The malleability of evil, of course, ranks among its most ancient features: Satan is the archetypal shape shifter. Yet, a postmodern perspective provides a major difference in viewing the malleability of evil as, at last, a cultural artifact. Moreover, the near identification between evil and suffering throws a new light onto suffering. Suffering, from a postmodern point of view, now appears not a permanent, ungraspable mystery of the human condition – something always enigmatic and beyond comprehension – but rather an event, even when locked within the privacy of an individual consciousness, that expresses much of what our cultures have taught us. In the extended social history of evil, one solid advantage that accrues to the postmodern moment lies in the implicit promise that we may, at least in part, address and redress the suffering that we have so thoroughly helped to shape. We may, unlike Adam, begin to turn towards the evil around us.

Notes

1 L. Kramer, "1,112 and Counting" (1983), *Reports from the Holocaust: The Making of an AIDS Activist*, New York, St Martin's Press, 1989, p. 33. For a critique of Kramer's manner as inadvertently reinforcing oppressive views of gays, see D. Bergman, "Larry Kramer and the Rhetoric of AIDS," *Gaiety Transfigured: Gay Self-Representation in American Literature*, Madison, University of Wisconsin Press, 1991, pp. 122–38.

2 See United States Public Health Service, "Public Health Service Plan for the Prevention and Control of AIDS and the AIDS Virus," *Public Health Reports*, July–August, 1996, pp. 341–48; and World Health Organization, *In Point of Fact*, no. 74, Geneva, WHO, 1991.

3 Kramer, *Reports from the Holocaust*, p. 145.

4 J. Derrida, "The Rhetoric of Drugs" (1989), trans. M. Israel, *Differences: A Journal of Feminist Cultural Studies*, 1993, vol. 5, no. 1, p. 20.

5 See *Personal Dispatches: Writers Confront AIDS*, J. Preston (ed.), New York, St Martin's Press, 1989; F. Brooks and T. F. Murphy, "Annotated Bibliography of AIDS Literature, 1982–91," *Writing AIDS: Gay Literature, Language, and Analysis*, T. F. Murphy and S. Poirier (eds), New York, Columbia University Press, 1993, pp. 321–39; and A. Hunsaker Hawkins, *Reconstructing Illness: Studies in Pathography*, West Lafayette, IN, Purdue University Press, 1993.

6 A. Juhasz, "Knowing AIDS through the Televised Science Documentary," *Women and AIDS: Psychological Perspectives*, C. Squire (ed.), Newbury Park, CA, Sage Publications, 1993, pp. 150–64. See also A. Juhasz and C. Saalfield, *AIDS TV: Identity, Community, and Alternative Video*, Durham, NC, Duke University Press, 1995. For early coverage of AIDS on British television, see S. Watney, "AIDS on Television," *Policing Desire: Pornography, AIDS, and the Media*, Minneapolis, University of Minnesota Press, 1987, pp. 97–122. For American television, see J. Kinsella, *Covering the Plague: AIDS and the American Media*, New Brunswick, NJ, Rutgers University Press, 1989; and two essays by P. A. Treichler, "AIDS Narratives on Television: Whose Story?," *Writing AIDS*, Murphy and Poirier (eds), pp. 161–99 and "Seduced and Terrorized: AIDS and Network Television," *A Leap in the Dark: AIDS, Art and Contemporary Cultures*, A. Klusacek and K. Morrison (eds), Montreal, Véhicule Press, 1992, pp. 136–51.

7 See J. Williamson, "Every Virus Tells a Story: The Meanings of HIV and AIDS," *Taking Liberties: AIDS and Cultural Politics*, E. Carter and S. Watney (eds), London, Serpent's Tail, 1989, pp. 69–80. Also, L. Edelman, "The Plague of Discourse: Politics, Literary Theory, and AIDS," *Displacing Homophobia: Gay Male Perspectives in Literature and Culture*, R. R. Butters, J. M. Clum, and M. Moon (eds), Durham, NC, Duke University Press, 1989, pp. 289–305; T. Yingling, "AIDS in America: Postmodern Governance, Identity, and Experience," *Inside/Out: Lesbian Theories, Gay Theories*, D. Fuss (ed.), New York, Routledge, 1991, pp. 291–310; and A. G. Düttmann, *At Odds with AIDS: Thinking and Talking About a Virus* (1993), trans. P. Gilgen and C. Scott-Curtis, Stanford, Stanford University Press, 1996.

8 S. L. Gilman, "The Beautiful Body and AIDS: The Image of the Body at Risk at

the Close of the Twentieth Century," *Picturing Health and Illness: Images of Identity and Difference*, Baltimore, MD, Johns Hopkins University Press, 1995, pp. 115–72.

9 See, in addition to her studies cited above (note 6), P. A. Treichler, "AIDS, Homophobia, and Biomedical Discourse: An Epidemic of Signification," *Cultural Studies*, 1987, vol. 1, no. 3, pp. 263–305; "AIDS, Gender, and Biomedical Discourse: Current Contests for Meaning," *AIDS: The Burdens of History*, E. Fee and D. M. Fox (eds), Berkeley, University of California Press, 1988, pp. 190–266; "AIDS, HIV, and the Cultural Construction of Reality," *The Time of AIDS: Social Analysis, Theory, and Method*, Newbury Park, CA, Sage Publications, 1992, pp. 65–98; and "How to Use a Condom: Bedtime Stories for the Transcendental Signifier," *Disciplinarity and Dissent in Cultural Studies*, C. Nelson and D. Parameshwar Gaonkar (eds), New York, Routledge, 1996, pp. 347–96. A collection of Treichler's work has been published recently in *How to Have Theory in an Epidemic: Cultural Chronicles of AIDS*, Durham, NC, Duke University Press, 1999.

10 J.-F. Lyotard, *The Postmodern Condition: A Report on Knowledge* (1979), trans. G. Bennington and B. Massumi, Minneapolis, University of Minnesota Press, 1984, pp. 34–7.

11 P. Ricoeur, *The Encyclopedia of Religion*, M. Eliade (ed.), New York, MacMillan, 1987, s.v. "evil." Ricoeur's text is based in part on his well-known study *The Symbolism of Evil*, trans. Emerson Buchanan, New York, Harper & Row, 1967.

12 A. Delbanco, *The Death of Satan: How Americans Have Lost the Sense of Evil*, New York, Farrar, Straus and Giroux, 1995.

13 See, for example, J. B. Russell, *The Devil: Perceptions of Evil From Antiquity to Primitive Christianity*, Ithaca, NY, Cornell University Press, 1977; J. S. Feinberg, *Theologies and Evil*, Washington, DC, University Press of America, 1979; M. Midgley, *Wickedness: A Philosophical Essay*, London and Boston, Routledge and Kegan Paul, 1984; J. T. Wilcox, *The Bitterness of Job: A Philosophical Reading*, Ann Arbor, University of Michigan Press, 1989; N. Noddings, *Women and Evil*, Berkeley, University of California Press, 1989; David Ray Griffin, *Evil Revisited: Responses and Reconsiderations*, Albany, State University of New York Press, 1991; and L. Watson, *Dark Nature: A Natural History of Evil*, New York, HarperCollins Publishers, 1995.

14 *Facing Evil: Light at the Core of Darkness*, P. Woodruff and H. A. Wilmer (eds), LaSalle, IL, Open Court, 1989.

15 H. Arendt, *Eichmann in Jerusalem: A Report on the Banality of Evil* (1963), revised and enlarged edition, New York, Viking Press, 1965. Arendt notes two "special qualities" – far from the traditional roots of evil – that Eichmann early discovered in himself: "he could organize and he could negotiate" (p. 45). On the decline and transformation of sin in the postmodern era, see J. N. Shklar, *Ordinary Vices*, Cambridge, MA, Harvard University Press, 1984.

16 See, for example, A. B. Pinn, *Why, Lord?: Suffering and Evil in Black Theology*, New York, Continuum, 1995.

17 T. Anders, *The Evolution of Evil: An Inquiry into the Ultimate Origins of Human Suffering*, Chicago, Open Court, 1994, p. 334. See also L. W. Doob, *Panorama of Evil: Insights from the Behavioral Sciences*, Westport, CO, Greenwood Press, 1978; and H. K. Bloom, *The Lucifer Principle: A Scientific Expedition into the Forces of History*, New York, Atlantic Monthly Press, 1995.

18 E. Levinas, "Useless Suffering" (1982), trans. R. Cohen, *The Provocation of Levinas: Rethinking the Other*, R. Bernasconi and D. Wood (eds), New York, Routledge, 1988, pp. 161–2.

19 Levinas, "Useless Suffering," p. 157.

20 Levinas, "Useless Suffering," p. 158.
21 Levinas, "Useless Suffering," p. 157.
22 Levinas, "Useless Suffering," p. 157.
23 A. Kleinman, V. Das, and M. Lock, "Introduction," *Social Suffering*, A. Kleinman, V. Das, and M. Lock (eds), Berkeley, University of California Press, 1997, p. ix.
24 Ricoeur, *Encyclopedia of Religion*, Eliade (ed.), p. 200.
25 See especially G. Gutiérrez, *A Theology of Liberation: History, Politics and Salvation* (1971), trans. Sister C. Inda and J. Eagleson, Maryknoll, NY, Orbis Books, 1973, and *On Job: God-Talk and the Suffering of the Innocent* (1985), trans. M. J. O'Connell, Maryknoll, NY, Orbis Books, 1987.
26 C. E. Rosenberg, *Explaining Epidemics and Other Studies in the History of Medicine*, Cambridge, Cambridge University Press, 1992, p. 292. On the distinctiveness of AIDS as a meta-disease, which attacks not specific organs or tissues but the immune system itself, see M. D. Grmek, *History of AIDS: Emergence and Origin of a Modern Pandemic* (1989), trans. R. C. Maulitz and J. Duffin, Princeton, NJ, Princeton University Press, 1990. For a critique of analogies that interpret AIDS through past plagues, as if AIDS were radically discontinuous with current patterns of disease, see E. Fee and D. M. Fox, "The Contemporary Historiography of AIDS," *Journal of Social History*, 1989, vol. 23, no. 2, pp. 303–14.
27 See, in addition to the work of Treichler (above), *AIDS: The Burdens of History*, E. Fee and D. M. Fox (eds), Berkeley, University of California Press, 1988; *AIDS: Cultural Analysis/Cultural Activism*, D. Crimp (ed.), Cambridge, MA, The MIT Press, 1988; *The Social Impact of AIDS in the U.S.*, R. A. Berk (ed.), Cambridge, MA, Abt Books, 1988; R. Byer, *Private Acts, Social Consequences: AIDS and the Politics of Public Health*, New York, Free Press, 1989; *Culture and AIDS*, D. A. Feldman (ed.), New York, Praeger, 1990; *AIDS and the Social Sciences*, R. Ulack and W. F. Skinner (eds), Lexington, The University Press of Kentucky, 1991; M. A. Muir, *The Environmental Context of AIDS*, New York, Praeger, 1991; *The Social Context of AIDS*, J. Huber and B. E. Schneider (eds), Newbury Park, CA, Sage Publications, 1992; M. Pollak with G. Paicheler and J. Pierret, *AIDS: A Problem for Sociological Research*, Newbury Park, CA, Sage Publications, 1992; and H. Fan, R. F. Conner, and L. P. Villarreal, *AIDS: Science and Society*, Boston, Jones and Bartlett, 1996.
28 S. Sontag, *AIDS and Its Metaphors*, New York, Farrar, Straus and Giroux, 1989, p. 17.
29 M. D. Quam, "The Sick Role, Stigma, and Pollution: The Case of AIDS," *Culture and AIDS*, Feldman (ed.), pp. 45–54. See also *Stigma and Sexual Orientation: Understanding Prejudice Against Lesbians, Gay Men, and Bisexuals*, G. M. Herek (ed.), Thousand Oaks, CA, Sage Publications, 1998.
30 S. C. McCombie, "AIDS in Cultural, Historic, and Epidemiologic Context," *Culture and AIDS*, Feldman (ed.), pp. 15–16.
31 P. E. Farmer, *AIDS and Accusation: Haiti and the Geography of Blame*, Berkeley, University of California Press, 1992. See also P. A. Treichler, "AIDS and HIV Infection in the Third World: A First World Chronicle," *Remaking History*, B. Kruger and P. Mariani (eds), Dia Art Foundation Discussions in Contemporary Culture, no. 4, Seattle, WA, Bay Press, 1989, pp. 31–86.
32 C. C. Taylor, "AIDS and the Pathogenesis of Metaphor," *Culture and AIDS*, Feldman (ed.), p. 58.
33 Quoted in M. Fisher, *I'll Not Go Quietly: Mary Fisher Speaks Out*, New York, Scribner, 1995, p. 92.
34 C. Patton, "'With Champagne and Roses': Women at Risk from/in AIDS Discourse," *Women and AIDS*, Squire (ed.), pp. 165–87; and J. Kitzinger, "Visible

and Invisible Women in AIDS Discourses," *AIDS: Setting a Feminist Agenda*, L. Doyal, J. Naidoo, and T. Wilton (eds), London, Taylor & Francis, 1994, pp. 95–109.

35 "The Denver Principles: Founding Statement of People with AIDS/ARC" (1983), The ACT UP/New York Women and AIDS Book Group, *Women, AIDS, and Activism*, Boston, South End Press, 1990, pp. 239–40.

36 R. Shilts, "AIDSpeak Spoken Here," *And the Band Played On: Politics, People, and the AIDS Epidemic*, New York, St Martin's Press, 1987, pp. 314–23. Shilts notes: "The new syntax allowed gay political leaders to address and largely determine public health policy in the coming years, because public health officials quickly mastered AIDSpeak, and it was fundamentally a political tongue" (p. 315).

37 M. Navarre, "Fighting the Victim Label," *AIDS: Cultural Analysis/Cultural Activism*, D. Crimp (ed.), Cambridge, MA, The MIT Press, 1988, p. 145. D. Crimp argues for the combination of mourning *and* activism ("Mourning and Militancy," *October* 51, 1989, pp. 3–18).

38 A. W. Frank, *The Wounded Storyteller: Body, Illness, and Ethics*, Chicago, University of Chicago Press, 1995, pp. 97–114.

39 J. Elsley, "The Rhetoric of the NAMES Project AIDS Quilt: Reading the Text(ile)," *AIDS: The Literary Response*, E. S. Nelson (ed.), New York, Twayne Publishers, 1992, pp. 187–96.

40 G. Woods, "AIDS to Remembrance: The Uses of Elegy," *AIDS: The Literary Response*, Nelson (ed.), pp. 155–66.

41 G. M. Carter, *ACT UP: The AIDS War & Activism*, Open Magazine Pamphlet Series, no. 15, Westfield, NJ, Open Media, 1992, p. 18.

42 Fan, Conner, and Villarreal, *AIDS: Science and Society*, pp. 204–5. See also G. Elbaz, *New York ACT UP*, Ph.D. dissertation, City University of New York, 1993. ACT UP also lobbied in a fairly traditional and effective manner for changes in government health-care policies.

43 J. M. Clum, "'And Once I Had It All': AIDS Narratives and Memories of an American Dream," *Writing AIDS*, Murphy and Poirier (eds), p. 220. This paragraph is indebted to Clum's account.

44 S. Aronowitz, "Against the Liberal State: ACT-UP and the Emergence of Postmodern Politics," *Social Postmodernism: Beyond Identity Politics*, L. Nicholson and S. Seidman (eds), Cambridge, Cambridge University Press, 1995, p. 361.

45 See A. Kleinman and J. Kleinman, "The Appeal of Experience; The Dismay of Images: Cultural Appropriations of Suffering in Our Times," *Social Suffering*, Kleinman, Das, and Lock (eds), pp. 1–23.

46 On moral community, see T. Regan, *The Thee Generation: Reflections on the Coming Revolution*, Philadelphia, PA, Temple University Press, 1991, p. 20.

Ethics

5 The Reflexivity of Evil[1]

Modernity and Moral Transgression in the War in Bosnia

Thomas Cushman

I

It is common practice in studies of evil to begin with an anecdote or story which tries to capture the essence of the evil under study. It is not easy to do this, in part because one runs the risk of reducing the immensity and complexity of evil to one image, and no one image can stand in for such immensity and complexity. But there are events which in their singularity capture the essence of a particular evil, which, in this essay, is the evil that occurred in Bosnia. Zlatko Dizdarević, a prominent Sarajevo writer whose articles about the siege of Sarajevo and the destruction of Bosnia are notable for the way they capture the grievousness and the absurdity of the destruction of Bosnia, writes:

> In Sarajevo a three-year-old girl playing outside her home is hit by a sniper's bullet. Her horrified father carries her to the hospital. Bleeding, she hovers between life and death. Only after her father, a big hulk of a man, has found a doctor to care for her does he allow himself to burst into tears. The television camera records his words. These words, every one of them, belong in an anthology of humanism, helplessness and forgiveness at its most extreme – not so much forgiving the criminal who shot a three-year-old child, as forgiving the wild beasts for *being* wild beasts, for being debased by an evil that destroys every human impulse. Two of his sentences accompany thoughts that will linger long past today or tomorrow. The first comes when the stricken father invites the unknown assassin to *have a cup of coffee with him so that he can tell him, like a human being, what has brought him to do such a thing*. Then he says, aware that this question might not elicit any *human response*: "One day, her tears will catch up with him . . ."[2]

What is significant about this story? One is tempted to begin with the analysis of the culture that could produce a man who could be so conciliatory and forgiving in the face of such wanton and intentional cruelty against his child. Yet it is the wanton cruelty of the act itself – the very evil of the assassination of a small, defenseless child – that most captures our attention. We, like the father, find the act incomprehensible and are left aghast by it. The father's question is a desperate and plaintive one, asked without expectation of an answer to the voyeuristic journalists who were an omnipresent part of the *mise-en-scène* of Bosnian misery. He, like we, realize that the answer to his question lies somewhere beyond the realm of rational explanation, in the realm of the irrational, unpredictable world of evil.

Or does it? There is an apocalyptic quality to much writing on Bosnia, a certain awestruck "homage to the extreme" as Michael Bernstein calls it, which presumes that the answers to the question "Why did it happen?" lie outside the ken of normal human knowledge.[3] Rather than assume that events in Bosnia reveal some greater metaphysical truth about evil or about some presumed stage of regression or apocalypse in Western culture, I suggest that there might be a way to offer at least some answer to the question of why those events occurred and that such an answer lies in the analysis of the discrete actions and interactions of specific agents within the contours of the social time and space in which such agents exist. In this essay, I would like to render the rhetorical question "Why did it happen?" into a sociological one: "What brought individual agents to do such things and how were their acts facilitated by their social and cultural environments?" The answer to this question requires a sociology of evil that does not really exist, or if it does, only exists inchoately in a few explicitly sociological works that attempt to present the logic of evil and cruelty. My central purpose here is to work toward the provision of such a theory. There are, to be sure, problems that immediately arise in such a task.

As a moral concept, evil is an "ancient, and heavily freighted term."[4] The freight, in this case, is the baggage of morality, metaphysics, emotions, essentialism, psychology – in short, all of the things that sociology has defined itself against in the course of its development as an autonomous discipline. Sociology is grounded in philosophy. But if philosophy prior to the twentieth century seemed inordinately concerned with the question of evil (as can be seen in the works of Hegel, Kant, Hume, and Schopenhauer, to name some of the most prominent), sociology is characterized by a conscious distancing of itself from the term and a selective appropriation of ideas that fit the nascent discipline's idea of human nature and the positive telos of human evolution. Indeed, evil is sociology's *Doppelgänger*, always present, but unwelcome, haunting the discipline and its quest for enlightenment by calling to mind questions of metaphysics, agency, and the "dark side" of human progress.

If evil appears at all in mainstream sociological theory, it does so as a "falling away" from the good. As Jeffrey Alexander notes: "In social scientific formulations of culture, a society's 'values' are studied primarily as orientations to the good, as efforts to embody ideals. Social notions of evil, badness, negativity are explored only as patterned departures from normatively regulated conduct."[5] And, as Niklas Luhmann tells us, it is

Durkheim's own sense of evil in his sociology that sets the pace for the career of the concept of evil in the development of sociology: evil, for Durkheim, is basically seen as the *absence* of the good instead of the *presence* of something unto itself.[6] Evil is always "not-A" rather than "A." This moral stance – the idea that immorality, deviance, and evil are "fallings away" from the good – is deeply embedded in the history of sociological thought and has worked to disestablish the ontological reality of evil in social theory and, by way of that, to elide the presence of evil in social life. If evil does appear as autonomous and independent reality, it does so as a *sense* of something negative about this or that social force rather than as an explicit quality of social forces. While purporting to be scientific and purely rational, such concepts as "*Gesellschaft,*" "*Entzauberung,*" "*anomie,*" or "*Kapital*" are axiological, conveying a negative sense of the world. While sociology aimed to set itself apart from the question of evil (a question that was central to philosophy), its concepts often convey a sense that, even if evil is not specifically addressed, it is still present in the world.

The first step in a sociology of evil, then, is to establish the ontological status of evil. Without such a status, there is only an emergent sociological evil or a purely relativistic conception, which makes it impossible to make any statements about the actual existence of something that we call evil.[7] Pragmatic philosophy and "social theory in the pragmatic mode" decry the effort to fix an idea of evil over and above the language which is used by human beings to describe the sensations they have of extreme phenomena. Yet after all that such philosophies and theories have said and done to distance themselves from the reality of evil, we are left – especially in consideration of the brutal facts of the twentieth century – with a sense that there are still things on earth that are not dreamt of in the philosophies of those whose business it is to know the world.

To do evil is to intentionally inflict excessive pain and suffering on someone else. What is evil about human actions is, in Abigail Rosenthal's words, "that aspect of them that intentionally obscures, disrupts, or deflects the ideal thread of plot in human lives" and which does so in a way that is, from a normative standpoint, excessive, cruel, or aberrant.[8] Neil Smelser notes that evil is "most appropriately applied to situations when force, violence, and other forms of coercion exceed institutional or moral limits."[9] John Kekes sees evil actions as those which "cause serious and morally unjustified harm to other human beings. [The] harm is serious if it interferes with the functioning of a person as a full-fledged agent."[10]

The second step in the sociology of evil is to raise the study of evil to a level on par with those of other phenomena usually studied by social scientists. Given the definition of evil offered above, it is easy to see why it is important to establish an operational idea of evil into the vocabulary of analysis of the destruction of Bosnia. It was a particularly cruel and ferocious event, one that was unimaginable in the context of late twentieth-century Europe. Yet, in the dominant discourse on the war, economic disparities, nationalism, historical precedent, and other background factors are usually offered as the explanatory variables that caused the war. These factors in and of themselves, though, cannot explain some of the most salient aspects of the war: the specific acts of barbarism and cruelty that characterize evil. Why did soldiers rape and kill wives and children in front of husbands and fathers and then leave the latter to live with the memory? Why did soldiers destroy beautiful and ancient architectural monuments which had no strategic value? Why were 8,000 people in Srebrenica told that they were to be evacuated and exchanged for prisoners of war and then machine-gunned and thrown in mass graves? Why were 12,000 people – 1,800 of whom were children – intentionally murdered in Sarajevo? The answers to these questions can never be found purely in the analysis of political, economic, or even cultural factors because, in the first instance, politics, economics, and culture never do anything by themselves. It is individuals who are enmeshed in politics, economics, and culture who do things through or in relation to politics, economics, and culture. That is to say, the true character of cruelty in Bosnia and Herzegovina (and I think of cruelty in general) is to be found in the *acts* of agents in relation to the structures that enable and constrain them.

At base, evil is *action* and, as such the theory of evil that I present here is a theory of action. It presents a view that contrasts with those accounts that rely on some kind of historical or cultural determinism to explain social outcomes in the Balkans: "The war was caused by age-old hatreds." "The Serbs are products of a cruel culture." "The Croats have a natural affinity for Nazism and genocide." These views constitute the main parameters of both popular and social science discourse on the war. They not only rely on crude stereotypes and errors of fact, but also fail to capture the sense of agency that is necessary in order to understand the specific qualities of evil and cruelty. One of the most important developments in contemporary social theory – especially theory that deals seriously with the issue of agency – is the idea that history and culture do not do anything by themselves. Rather, it is individuals who do things with the culture and history that surround them: "Men make history, but not in circumstances of their own choosing." It was individuals who destroyed Bosnia and they did so not as automatons or dupes of historical or cultural forces, but as willful agents who reflexively responded to the contours of both local and global history, who reflexively adapted themselves to the exigencies and contingencies of the unfolding present, and who reflexively presented an ideal vision of the future that their actions would, ideally, bring about.

II

While I want to develop a sociology of evil by way of reclaiming what is important from the philosophy of evil, I do want to distance myself from the idea of essential evil. The basis for a sociology of evil is not metaphysics, but theories of social action. Evil is not an essential quality of human beings, but is *intentional action*, the result of the conscious reflection of actors and the willful decision to do something severe to someone else. There is nothing terribly new about this idea. Most major theologians and philosophers who have dealt with the problem of evil have tied the latter directly and un- conditionally to the idea of free will. Augustine, Kant, Hegel, Nietzsche, and Schopenhauer, despite their many differences, shared this view, and I think that anyone would be hard-pressed to find such a strong point of agreement on any other substantive issue among these disparate thinkers.

If evil is agentic and intentional action that is reflexively chosen, it should be fairly easy to account for it from the standpoint of existing sociological theories of action and agency. We could just adapt the latter to interpret actions that we consider evil. Yet, sociological theorists of agency have, like sociological theorists in general, displaced evil. This displacement has much to do with the unbridled political optimism of the progenitors of the prag- matic theories of social action. William James made some space for the idea of evil, noting in *The Varieties of Religious Experience* that: "The normal process of life contains moments as bad as any of those which insane melancholy is filled with, moments in which radical evil gets its innings and takes its solid turns."[11] Yet James's sociological interpreters such as Mead and Cooley simply ignored the idea that the pragmatic, reflexive self could engage in action that was ferocious, malicious, and cruel in its ends, genesis, or outcomes. Action and reflexivity was, for these thinkers and their later followers, always considered as progressive. This development was ironic since such theories developed in a world historical context in which it was rather evident that agents used the infrastructure of modernity for nefarious rather than progressive ends.

This belief in the optimistic and moral ends of agency is very clear in the work of Anthony Giddens, perhaps the most prominent contemporary theorist of agency. For Giddens, agency is what drives the "life politics" that aim to reenchant a world disenchanted by modernity. If there is any evil embedded in Giddens' theory, it lies in his conception of modernity as a "juggernaut."[12] Agency, in contrast, expresses itself in the life projects of countermodernity. In Giddens' actor it is much more possible to see a saint than a sinner. As with Durkheim and Parsons, Giddens simply cannot imagine that, as Jeffrey Alexander notes, "evil might be valued as energetic- ally as the good."[13] This line of thought is carried forth in most sociological work that stresses agency and seems to be an essential political precondition for such theories.[14]

There is no logical or empirical reason to assume that reflexivity is fundamentally oriented to optimistic, progressive, Enlightenment ends. Indeed, if we are interested in looking at the ways in which agency is enabled by the infrastructures of modernity, we are likely to find our best examples in those whose acts would be classified as "transgressive." The archetypal, ideal-type model of the evil agent is to be found in the fictional characters of James Bond stories: brilliant geniuses who have mastered modern technologies in the service of grand anti-Enlightenment schemes. Such characters are highly reflexive agents, perhaps even hyperreflexive. But the ends of their agency and reflection are to maximize the pain and suffering of others, to deliberately obscure the plot lines of others' lives through creative intervention. This conception, of course, involves a break with the view that reflexivity and moral progress go hand in hand: reflexivity, in my view, is neither moral nor immoral, progressive nor regressive, modern nor barbaric by nature. Rather, evil is reflexive, creative, imaginative, adaptive, and cunning, whatever its axiological ends, and especially so in relation to the more technologically complex condition of modernity.[15] To miss or underestimate the reflexivity of evil is, I think, to fail to capture the most essential quality of evil.

So what we need is a conception of agency that allows us to examine evil as a form of social action. Such a conception can be found in an imaginative article on the nature of agency by Mustafa Emirbayer and Ann Mirsch, in which they note that agency always proceeds in relation to past, present, and future:

> Actors are always living simultaneously in the past, the future, and present, and adjusting to the various temporalities of their empirical existence to one another (and to their empirical circumstances) in more or less imaginative or reflective ways. They continuously engage in patterns and repertoires from the past, project hypothetical pathways forward in time, and adjust their actions to the exigencies of emerging situations.[16]

This "relational pragmatics," as the authors refer to it, allows us to conceive of agency as a function of a reflexive consciousness that is oriented toward three temporal planes: past, present, and future. The latter constitute a kind of "chordal triangle" which actors "play" as they engage in reflexive social action.

In stressing the temporal bases of action, Emirbayer and Mirsch's approach is much more sophisticated than that found in most theories of agency and offers an imaginative basis for examining the specific actions of agents under specific conditions of social time and space. Their view is also especially useful for understanding agency in the postmodern world in which past, future, and present are made manifest to actors in many more ways, through many different media. Curiously, though, the authors note that their analysis only delineates the "analytical space within which reflective and morally responsible action might be said to unfold."[17] There is no inherent reason why "relational pragmatics" should be considered inherently positive and morally responsible. Indeed, it is the central point of the present analysis that pragmatics are oriented in what might be called, to invert Emirbayer and Mirsch's terminology, "morally irresponsible ways." The connection between agency and moral responsibility is not grounded in an empirical assessment of the range of human activities, but rather is a product of the homage to the idealism of pragmatic social theory. It is, in fact, deceiving to restrict the analysis of action to those projects that are thought to be morally constructive and progressive. The destruction of Bosnia is only one recent case that illustrates that the forging of un-democratic politics, the perpetration of cruel and ferocious acts, and the masking of all the latter by the perpetrators and social science interpreters is the product of highly reflexive agents who insert themselves into the past, adapt to the present, and imagine a future. Such cruelty does not just happen; it is made.

III

The foregoing theoretical prolegomenon is meant to offer a basis for the analysis of key agents who set the stage for and committed acts of intentional cruelty in Bosnia. It is these acts which, taken cumulatively and collectively, constitute the destruction of Bosnia. Atrocities and cruelties were perpetrated by all sides, but the vast majority of atrocities and war crimes were committed by those on the Serbian side. Thus, I wish to focus principally on the Serbian elites who, as agents, set the historical process of the destruction of Bosnia into motion.[18]

There is a saying in the Serbo-Croatian language: "*riba se truje od glave nadolje*," which means that "fish rots from the head down." The principle architects of the destruction of Bosnia – Slobodan Milošević, Radovan Karadžić, Ratko Mladić, and Zeljko Raznjatović – set into motion a whole process, a whole machinery of agents who, *in toto*, effected the destruction of Bosnia. The Bosnian war was perhaps the most widely covered war in history; phalanxes of journalists were constantly on the scene to capture events as they unfolded. The presence of these journalists was a major factor in the reflexive considerations of the perpetrators of violence, and it is through these media that we can witness the destruction of Bosnia and the reflexive accounts of the agents who effected that destruction and provided a rationale for them. My data is the actual footage of these figures by Western journalists and the "presentations of self" that these elites put forth through local and global media. The words of these agents provide indications of the ways in which they consciously and reflexively played the past, present, and future as the basis for their ongoing social actions. I turn first to the principal agent in the dissolution of Bosnia, Slobodan Milošević.

Slobodan Milošević did not create himself as a nationalist, but actually inserted himself into an existing historical current of Serbian concern about the encroachment of national minorities on Serbs, particularly in the autonomous region of Kosovo. The special importance of Kosovo as the place where the Serbs suffered defeat at the hands of the "Turks" in 1389 is quite well known. But all through Serbian history, Kosovo has been a special site of tension between Albanians and Serbs: this tension had been exacerbated in the nineteenth and twentieth centuries by patterns of out-migration of Serbs and in-migration of Albanians. Obsessive concern with this process was a hallmark of Serbian nationalist programs. In 1937, in an address to the Serbian Culture Club in Belgrade (and later deposited in an archive of the Yugoslav National Army), Vasa Čubrilović, a professor at the University of Belgrade, provided a stark plan for the forced deportation, terrorization, and recolonization of the southern lands of Serbia, which included Kosovo.[19]

In his address, Čubrilović outlines the history of Albanian "penetration" into the lands of southern Serbia. He notes that this "Albanian bloc" cuts off the northern parts of Serbia from strategically important access to southern rivers and seas. The simple solution is the removal of the Albanian population by the use of force. He writes:

> Our first task is not to leave a land of such strategic importance in the hands of an alien and hostile nation.... We cannot succeed in suppressing Albanians only by gradual colonization because they are the only nation that has managed to survive within the nucleus of our state... but also to push our ethnic borders back towards the north and east in the last millennium.... The only solution is to use brute force. We have always been superior to them in its use.[20]

After noting that the trend of Albanian encroachment into Serbia can only get worse due to the exceptional fertility of Albanian women relative to Serbian women, Čubrilović provides a detailed plan for the forcible eviction "en masse" of the Albanian population to lands in Albania and Turkey and the repopulation of the ethnically cleansed areas with Serbs. His plan has many of the trimmings of other blueprints for ethnic cleansing in the twentieth century – an organized program of terror, the use of brute strength to force emigration, and the willful destruction of the "foreign" culture. Čubrilović minces no words: "To cause the massive emigration, the first prerequisite is to generate fear" and to use the "pressure of the state apparatus" which

> should make the Albanian existence here as bitter as possible: fines, arrests, ruthless application of all the police sanctions, punishments for smuggling, hewing down, and letting dogs loose, enforcing statute labor and all the other methods at the disposal of the police.[21]

This plan of terror and force is all to be followed by a repopulation of southern lands under the direction of the Serbian Royal Academy of Science in Belgrade and Čubrilović's colleagues at the University of Belgrade whose scientific and objective studies of the problem would be the basis for the formation of a "Colonization Institute," whose task it would be to develop and implement techniques for eviction and resettlement.

This motif ran through twentieth-century Serbian history and found expression and intensification in later pronouncements of Serbian intellectuals. In January 1986, two hundred prominent Belgrade intellectuals signed a petition to the Yugoslav and Serbian national assemblies.[22] This petition laments the "genocide" of the Serbian people and demands the

> right to spiritual identity, to defense of the foundations of Serb national culture and to the physical survival of our nation on its land. We demand decisive measures, and that the concern and will of all Yugoslavia be mobilized in order to stop the Albanian aggression in Kosovo and Metohija.[23]

The petition was signed by notable intellectuals, including former "Marxist humanist" editors of the prominent Yugoslav Marxist journal *Praxis*: Zaga Golubović, Mihailo Marković, and Ljubomir Tadić. The alignment of these prominent intellectuals with aggressive nationalism not only puzzled left acolytes of Yugoslav Marxism, but also pointed to a close connection between the latter and nationalism that has often been elided in contemporary accounts. In a later pronouncement on February 26, 1987, the three editors published a rejoinder to a criticism by Michele Lee of their support of nationalism.[24] While claiming to continue to uphold the principles of democratic socialism in the journal and the general rights of all minorities, the three editors stress that, as Serbs, they are also defending the "Serbian victims of oppression."[25] They refer to the Albanian people as the "little David" which

> always had the upper hand most of the time because it was amply supported by overwhelming allies: the Islamic Ottoman Empire during five centuries until 1912; Austria Hungary which occupied the entire territory during World War I; fascist Italy and Germany which did the same during World War II; the Soviet Union and China after 1948; eventually a dominating anti-Serbian coalition itself over the last twenty years.[26]

Notice in this description the highly relational articulation of Serbian victimization: it emerges through the long durée of the history of domination of foreign peoples by enemies of all ideological stripes and continues to this day, ostensibly embodied in the nascent movements for autonomy taking place in other parts of Yugoslavia. The past is always present and all the more so in the most reflexive elements of the population, namely, the intellectuals.

These contours of Serbian history formed the central aspect of the more general cultural milieu in which political leaders in the disintegrating Yugoslavia existed. Serbian history really was characterized by the series of oppressions named. What was decisive for the fate of Bosnia was the ways in which this history was "played" by politicians in the present. No one was a more skillful player than Milošević; his very power depended fundamentally on his exploitation and intensification of these anti-Albanian sentiments and the perception of the danger posed by Albanians to the Serbs. Indeed, what is remarkable about the tense situation in Kosovo, both in the late 1980s and now, is the way in which the present-day Albanians are seen as "Turk-surrogates," symbolic stand-ins for the real Turks who defeated Prince Lazar 600 years before in 1389 at the Battle of Kosovo. In terms of the temporal plane of history, what distinguishes so much of the social action in the Balkans is the way in which history resides so close to the surface, always ready to be taken into consideration as the justification for this or that act in the present. Milošević set the stage for this contemporaneization of history in a famous speech to Kosovo Polje on April 24, 1987. Milošević used the tensions in Kosovo to effect a transformation of his own political identity from a communist apparatchik to nationalist "savior of the Serbian people." This was a highly intentional act, and while it no doubt "brewed" for some time, we have actual footage that shows the exact moment when Milošević recreated his identity.

The Kosovo gathering shows the volatile mix of crowd dynamics, political calculations, the construction of charisma, and conscious insertion of the self into history that comprise acts of agency in the Balkans. While it is clear that Milošević emerged victorious at this time, what is not often commented on is the high degree of contingency and unpredictability of this event. Like other reflexive interactions in situations of co-presence, the interactions of a political leader with the masses is a precarious endeavor, even more so perhaps since the reflexivity of the "mob" is not highly developed and, thus, the leader is forced to play to the mob rather than the other way around. Milošević might well have emerged a villain rather than a hero, and the contingency of the event is evident in the way the situation played itself out. While the event was highly orchestrated, the leader seemed ever conscious of the precariousness of the situation and only "struck" when he was sure that the identity he had chosen would resonate with the crowd. It might just as well have gone the other way.

Milošević's declaration, "You will not be beaten again," is an utterance which places him, at once, in the past, present, and future: the reference to "again" does not refer to the immediate past of the staged and contrived attack on Serbs outside the lecture hall just a few moments ago, but to the long-standing beating of the Serbs by Albanians which has, presumably, occurred since 1389. The utterance itself is a reflexive orientation to the mob which, in the present, demands something immediate of Milošević, and the use of the future tense means that Milošević has defined a vision of the future in which the Serbs will be safe from other threats. While I would not like to make too much out of one utterance, I would say that the pattern of "playing" the chordal triangle of past, present, and future which is so evident in this utterance was to establish itself as the principle grounding for destructive acts in Bosnia.

Milošević continued this playing of past, present, and future as he assumed more power. On May 8, 1989, Milošević assumed the presidency of Yugoslavia. The next month, on June 28, again at the very battlefield where the "Turks" had defeated the Serbs, a mass rally of over one million people was staged. Milošević as the transformed Serbian nationalist leader played the key role in the spectacle, which took place at Gazimestan, at the actual site of the battle of Kosovo. Mass audiences were convened to greet Milošević who, just as Hitler had descended to Nuremberg sixty years before in an airplane, descended to the field in a helicopter to greet the people. This spectacle continued Milošević's reflexive transformation of his own identity. I want to stress this because, for the purpose of my general argument here, history is not simply a background force that caused the dissolution of Yugoslavia and the attendant destruction of Bosnia: it was a force that was *activated* by agents to refashion their identities and, by way of that, to alter the specific contours of the present and future. His speech elaborated the major motifs of Serbian propaganda that legitimated the war that was to follow: the Serbs are never aggressors; they are "liberators" who try to help others and who are thwarted in this by the aggressive and thankless hostility of those others:

> Serbs in their history have never conquered or exploited others. Through two world wars, they have liberated themselves and, when they could, they also helped others to liberate themselves.... The Kosovo heroism does not allow us to forget that at one time we were brave and dignified and one of the few who went into battle undefeated.... Six centuries later, again we are in battles and quarrels. They are not armed battles, though such things should not be excluded yet.[27]

The consideration of Milošević as a reflexive agent is not meant to decide the question about whether or not Milošević is actually "evil" in some essential sense, although the case could be made philosophically that he is wicked, that is, he is an individual who is an "habitual evildoer."[28] The point is that in his actions we see a strong intersection between the reflexive remaking of Milošević's self and the investing of that self into a series of social actions that had a specific effect on the present and Serbian future. If it is the case that Milošević's actions in the beginning of the war were the pretext for the destruction of Bosnia, it is also the case that his own actions enabled others who were the executors of his plans for the forcible repression of newly independent states of the former Yugoslavia. While Milošević's transformation set the ball in motion, there is a seeming inconsistency between Milošević's rather dispassionate and bureaucratic demeanor and the events that have come to characterize the war in ex-Yugoslavia: the brutal rapes, the acts of torture and mutilations, the killing of civilians and non-combatants. It is very easy to see Machiavelli rather than Rousseau in him.

Yet Milošević's own transformation set in motion a general movement away from pure Machiavellianism to a more "fragrant," contractual, and aestheticized version of transgression – transgression that manifested itself almost as a kind of Durkheimian ritual of negative solidarity. We can move from the analysis of the reflexive self of a former communist party leader who turned nationalist for his own benefit to the analysis of the true believers who precipitated acts of cruelty in the name of the nation, the self-defense of the victimized Serbian people. In such a movement, we see manifestations of an autonomous evil, in which agents such as Milošević are well aware of what they are doing, and what John Kekes calls non-autonomous evil, in which actors perpetrate evil acts, but are convinced that what they are doing is good, righteous, or just.[29] Whether autonomous or non-autonomous, like Milošević, these same actors played the chordal triangle of past, present, and future as they committed their acts of transgression.

Nowhere was this enthusiastic transgression more clear than in the case of General Ratko Mladić. In January 1991, Mladić was the deputy commander of the army corps in the province of Kosovo and later, in 1992, became the military commander of the Bosnian Serb forces. Mladić, who had close ties with Milošević, is one of the agents who bears primary responsibility for the destruction of Bosnia; indeed, he has been indicted by the International War Crimes Tribunal for the crime of genocide and crimes against humanity. The list of crimes in the indictment include setting up detention facilities; targeting political leaders, intellectuals, and professionals; deporting Bosnian Muslims and Bosnian Croats; shelling civilian gatherings; appropriating and plundering property; destroying property; and destroying sacred sites.[30] According to one journalist:

> By his own account, Ratko Mladić is a student of Hannibal, Alexander the Great and Carl von Clausewitz. But over the last three years, in battle after battle, he has shown his belief in the doctrine of concentrated force espoused by Heinz Guderian, the German panzer general: Klotzen, nicht Kleckern! – "Smash! Don't sprinkle!" Mladić's commands to his artillery units around Sarajevo included: "Roast!" "Pound them senseless!"[31]

Like Milošević, Mladić grounded his acts of destruction in the chordal triad of past, present, and future. Such acts were immediately grounded in a sense of Serbian history, a history that was always flush with the present. Consider the destruction of Srebrenica, the supposed UN safe area – Mladić is known for his central role in this event which is now considered to be the worst atrocity of the entire war and, indeed, the worst atrocity to occur in Europe since the end of the Second World War.[32] Mladić, the commander and chief of the Bosnian Serb forces, led the assault on Srebrenica. The assault was a highly reflexive act; indeed, it played itself out precisely in relation to the responses of the West, which were carefully monitored by Mladić's forces. Jan Honig and Norbert Booth describe the way in which practically every Serbian military action played itself out with specific, calculated references to global actors. Such actors were seldom physically present, but they were omnipresent in the minds of the perpetrators as they reflexively considered the possibilities for social action:

> After gaining new ground the Serbs would invariably pause. With so many UN Troops and observers present, they had to be wary of a possible international armed response. A pause enabled them to gauge the world's reaction. Also, it tended to make the attack appear like a limited or isolated incident – a moment of pique that would not continue. They usually succeeded in taking the sting out of any intended tough response.[33]

This ongoing articulation of action with the ongoing present involved an almost constant interaction of Mladić and others with the agents who possessed the means to "make or break" the Serbs. Thus it was that Mladić was able to present himself to people such as General Michael Rose, the commander of UN forces in Bosnia, even as he was planning the liquidation of Muslims from the safe area of Srebrenica. In such interactions, if visual images are any evidence, Mladić was able to convince Rose that he was not so bad after all and had legitimate military objectives and the means to achieve them.

In addition to this reflexive consideration of the present, what was also important was the way in which the past lurked near the surface of the present. The case of Milošević's rise to power seems relatively benign when considered against the actions of Mladić in his concrete military campaigns of ethnic cleansing. According to Mark Danner, upon conquering Srebrenica, Mladić spoke to the television camera:

> Here we are in Srebrenica on July 11, 1995. On the eve of yet another great Serbian holiday, we present this city to the Serbian people as a gift. Finally, after the rebellion of the Dahijas, the time has come to take revenge on the Turks of this region.[34]

Again, the Muslim residents of Srebrenica are linked unproblematically to a distant "Turkish" past, an event at Dahijas almost three hundred years before in which Turks ruthlessly suppressed a rebellion by Serbs in the region. This linkage grounded Mladić's perpetration of his own atrocity in the present. The atrocity itself is fundamentally tied to a vision of the future that is "Turk-less." Unlike Milošević's acts in Kosovo, which merely ignited the war, Mladić's acts constituted the war itself and they were a product of his reflexive consideration of past, present, and future.

Another key agent of destruction who gained a notable reputation for cruelty in the war was Zeljko Raznjatović. Raznjatović, who went by the nickname of "Arkan" and who was recently assassinated in Belgrade, emerged as a leader of the paramilitary organization Serbian Volunteer Guard, also known as the Tigers. Arkan emerged on the scene in the destruction and looting of the Croatian city of Vukovar in the fall of 1991. The destruction of Vukovar was what might be called, in modern capitalist parlance, a "market-testing exercise" in which the pattern of bouncing images out on the world and escalating violence in relation to the reception was established. Arkan later applied that same strategy in the destruction of towns and cities in Bosnia. There, his troops were photographed committing vicious atrocities against Muslim populations. Serbs from the very beginning recognized that their actions had to be reflexively tailored to the response of the Western "other," which was the primary recipient of the images of mass destruction. What is remarkable is that the images, sometimes consciously crafted to be transgressive, evoked very little response in the West, except for non-response and indifference, which themselves are a type of response. When such indifference was conveyed back to Serbian elites, this indifference itself was a significant gesture that enabled further acts of destruction. This "conversation of gestures," to use George Herbert Mead's terminology, was not simply the innocent basis of social life, but an active process that led to acts of extreme cruelty.

Western passivity in the face of the media images of the war was actually an active force because it clued in Serbian forces to the fact that they could engage in future destructive action with impunity. As the war progressed, these interaction rituals between agents of destruction and media became a permanent part of the landscape and a major means which allowed suspected war criminals not only to engage with Western audiences, but to provide a discursive ground for their actions. In these regularized media events, figures such as Arkan could articulate their own rationale and programs.

This interaction with the media allowed for the overt denial of actions or reconstruction of the identity of the perpetrators even in the face of the evidence for atrocity, which might occur even in the same clip. Arkan appears as a boyish, suave, sophisticated man who presents himself as a "gentlemanly defender of Serbian victims" even as he is surrounded by the evidence of mass destruction for which he and his soldiers appear to be responsible. Acts of intentional cruelty in the present are justified as acts of self-defense against an omnipotent historical other, and this discourse serves to deny and suppress the actual evidence of the evil of the event. While I have not focused on the mind of the Western audience, it is worthwhile to point out that the presentation of such contradictory images did not lead to action on the part of Western observers to stop aggression. Rather, it is more likely that it led to doubt and confusion as to what was actually going on. The "positive" messages which Arkan intentionally crafted in these little media spectacles – the facade of boyish charm, his facility with English, his association with the Serbian Orthodox Church, the reasonable-sounding story of the victimization of the Serbian people – contradict the historical reality and truth of the banal reality of evil. As the war progressed, it became progressively more difficulty to link the perpetrators of violence to the actual acts they had perpetrated because the reflexive and creative messages of the perpetrators did not resonate with the banality of the events that they were meant to mask.

Arkan's reflexive playing of the media was a pattern followed by all of the principal agents in the war. The latter were offered unprecedented opportunities to air their views in the major media venues of the West. At one point in the war, this mediated interaction between Western audiences and the perpetrators of the destruction of Bosnia reached a crescendo when Radovan Karadžić, the leader of the Bosnian Serbs, appeared on the CBS television news program "Sixty Minutes."[35] Karadžić, a former psychiatrist and poet, was the principal architect of the war and the principal ideologist of the Bosnian Serb position. He was offered a platform for his views on one of the most watched television shows in the United States. From a formal standpoint, this event was a case in which the leader most responsible for the war and the atrocities that occurred there could engage with Western audiences and present an account and rationale for his actions. This account served to deny his role in the atrocities in Bosnia by redefining and redescribing those events in terms of history, the present, and the future.

One of the major lines of thought in Karadžić's interview is the idea of the duplicity and untrustworthiness of Muslims. Karadžić puts forth the idea that the Muslims were so duplicitous that they actually shelled themselves in order to gain Western sympathy. And he notes that Muslims are characterized by "intolerance, torture, anxiety, and deception" and therefore, "I can't trust the Muslims because I have seen what they do to my people." One can imagine that this would play particularly well in a Western public infused with orientalist images of fundamentalist Muslims who commit acts of treachery. Indeed, Karadžić notes that "for some nations we are heroes, Russians, Rumanians, Bulgarians, Greeks" – all nations, incidentally, which have long histories of tensions with Turkish and Muslim peoples. In noting that Serbs are doing "the same thing they did to us during Second World War," Karadžić actually admits to atrocity, but conveys the idea that it is justified on the grounds of collective, historical guilt. Karadžić also notes that the Western media pays no attention to atrocities against Serbs, thus inferring that there is some kind of a conspiracy against Serbs. Finally, in the interview, Karadžić simply denies that there were any atrocities or crimes against humanity committed by his forces: "there were no killings except during fighting"; "my army and police have never committed any rape or atrocities." He even defends Ratko Mladić as a hero and denies the facts of Srebrenica. Toward the end of the interview, Mike Wallace notes: "I don't sense that there are any heroes in the Balkans." To which Karadžić replies: "You are right because what we are going to be can't be defined right now.

Time has to decide whether we are going to be heroes or criminals."
Karadžić ends his interview sounding the note of future orientation – the
actions that occurred in Bosnia were not only reflexively oriented toward the
past, played out in the context of an ever-shifting and highly mediated
present, but guided by a vision of the European future in which the Bosnian
Serbs would be redefined as the protectors of the cultural purity of Europe.
For Karadžić, what "we Serbs" are now is what others will think about us
in the future. He actually imagines himself a European hero and such an
imagining is not necessarily out of keeping within the long durée of European treatment of Muslims.[36]

I would argue that this interview is itself a model case which shows how
evil plays itself out in the postmodern world. It is far more than a thrust and
parry on television seen by millions of people: it is what might be called the
postmodern presentation of self, the reflexive playing of past, present, and
future through an omnipresent media that provides the raw material for a vast
audience of observers. Cruelty, torture, and heinous acts are not new in the
twentieth century; what is new is the way in which these things come to be
grounded in a new, mediated, dialectical relationship between the perpetrators of evil and observers. In this dialectic, the point of view of the
perpetrator has the possibility of appearing reasonable and understandable
and can then be inserted into any number of other discourses and presented
as a plausible and valid account. There is no idea in any of the accounts
presented above, whether those of Milošević, Mladić, Arkan, or Karadžić,
that cannot be found in the point of view of many Western intellectuals
or journalists who covered and interpreted the war. This "resonance of discourses" is relevant to the study of evil, for it is a resonance that elides the evil
that is itself elided and masked in the reflexive discourse of the perpetrator.

IV

I have made mention of the fact that the destruction of Bosnia was closely
watched by those in the West who also attempted to make meaning of the
events that happened there. In the last section of this essay, I want to raise
the issue of the Western response to the war in Bosnia in terms of the
relevance of that response for masking and eliding evil. The central contours
of the phenomenology of Western perception of the war were forged by the
constant presence of Western observers on the scene in Bosnia and the
constant interaction of the Western observers with the major and minor
players in that scene. But contrary to the idea that knowledge of an event
produces action in relation to it, the destruction of Bosnia was characterized
by a high degree of indifference on the part of the West toward events there.
The destruction of Bosnia was perhaps the most observed, covered, and
written about event in the history of the twentieth century, but this coverage
did not lead in any direct way to intervention to stop the events that were

occurring. In fact, as I have argued in the previous section, the vast media coverage actually was the necessary condition which allowed agents to play the chordal triangle of past, present, and future as they committed their acts of destruction. Thus it was, to extend Marx's famous insight, that men made history in circumstances that enabled them to reflect on it and present it to others in ways hitherto unimaginable until the advent of late modernity (or postmodernity, depending on one's preference for defining the epoch).

Many separate issues arise in considering this relationship: the extent to which the indifference was functional for Western observers, the extent to which such indifference was actually complicitous in the destruction of Bosnia, and the extent to which Western accounts of the war masked or elided the specific qualities of the war. That the West was complicitous in the destruction of Bosnia is true beyond a shadow of a doubt. From the very beginning of the war, the agents who committed the destruction of Bosnia took their cues from Western leaders: the information "given off," in Erving Goffman's sense, served as a reference point for reflection and for the commission of acts of ferocious cruelty.[37]

This is where we come to what is "postmodern" about the practice of evil as I have described it in this essay. My argument here is provocative: the amount of information and its mode of presentation meant that competing narratives of the war, narratives which defined the truth of the war in radically different ways, came to delineate the space of analysis. This is certainly natural given that an expanded public sphere is one of the defining characteristics of a pluralistic society. Yet, in this case, the media was actually central to the purpose of the actors justifying and masking their accounts of mass atrocity. The media maintained a certain "discursive solidarity" with the perpetrators of evil whom I discussed previously. It provided a space in which Radovan Karadžić, Slobodan Milošević, Ratko Mladić, and Arkan could, in an ongoing way, reflect on and construct a rationale for their actions, in the terms of my analysis here, to play the chordal triangle of past, present, and future to a vast audience of observers. The sounds of this concert were, in a sense, "products" for consumption by Western audiences.

It is so often said that "there is no real truth about the Balkan war," and it might be that, ironically, the truth of the event receded in proportion to the increase in the media coverage of the war. The media served to create a situation in which a set of competing vocabularies of motive could be presented. None of these vocabularies had any ontological or axiological primacy over the others. Indeed, since the presentation of accounts was not simply the presentation of truth-claims, but the persuasive rhetorics, gestures, and other symbolic tactics, the perpetrators had the constant opportunity to present their rationale for the torture. In the mind of the viewer – especially those for whom the apprehension of Bosnia was a completely mediated event – the reasonableness and seeming civility presented in a tactical mix of persuasive gestures could easily relegate the pain and torture for which the perpetrator was responsible to the margins of consciousness.

Thus, what one remembers about Ratko Mladić is not his ferocity or his commands to "roast" Muslim civilians, but his own pain as a victim of the Ustasha fascists in the Second World War. What one remembers about Radovan Karadžić is not that he gave the orders to murder children in Sarajevo, but his compelling, emotional, and vitally powerful historical story about the historical ill-treatment of the Serbs at the hands of people of Muslim and Croatian background. What one remembers about Slobodan Milošević is his facility with English, his seeming charm and reasonableness, and not the conscious inciting of hatred at Kosovo or the fact that he gave specific orders for the destruction of Vukovar. The events that defined the cruel character of the war receded the more the presentation of self of the agents who committed the acts was effected through the forms of mass media. The media offered the means for local actors to insert their vocabularies of motive into the global scene, to compete for the attention of the audience, and at least to create an idea of doubt about the truth of the war.

Elaine Scarry, in her seminal work on torture, notes that the structure of torture consists of three elements: the infliction of pain, the objectification of the subjective attribution of pain, and the translation of the objectified attributes of pain into the insignia of power. [38] This latter step, the denial of pain, is a consequence of the mass mediation of the Bosnian war, its transformation into a spectacle of competing accounts. In the acts of reflection and explanation that comprised the media spectacle, those who perpetrated the torture of Bosnia were able to deny the pain of that torture. There is, in Scarry's conception, a kind of cruelty to the very process of describing cruelty itself: the torturer first "inflicts pain, then objectifies pain, then denies pain – and only this final act of self-blinding permits the shift back to the first step, the inflicting of still more pain."[39] What is most important in the process of injury is the way in which injury achieves invisibility; this is done by a willful act of "omission" and "redescription":

> Redescription may . . . be understood as only a more active form of omission; rather than leaving out the fact of bodily damage, that fact is itself included and actively cancelled out as it is introduced into the spoken sentence or begins to be recorded on a written page. Alternatively, omission may be understood as only the most successful or extreme form of redescription where the fact of injury is now so successfully enfolded within the language that we cannot even sense its presence beneath the surface of that language.[40]

Scarry's observations about the discursive "disappearing" of pain describe well the actions of the agents involved in the destruction of Bosnia. It was through the postmodern plethora of media channels that the perpetrators of mass atrocities were able to commit acts of secondary symbolic violence: the disappearing, masking, and redescription of the pain and suffering of their victims through the propagation and dissemination of a welter of myths about the Serbian past, present, and future.

V

In his work *Lectures on the Philosophy of World History*, Hegel noted, quite rightly, that "it is in world history that we encounter the sum total of concrete evil." He was wrong, however, to surmise that the ultimate design of the world has been realized and that "evil has not been able to maintain a position of equality beside it."[41] Nowhere is the fact that we have not approached the "end of history" more evident than in Bosnia: the post-modern world, with its swirl of accounts, each circulating through the plethora of media outlets and each sounding as plausible and true as the other, has actually set the stage for the enabling of extreme behavior. The late twentieth century has become, in David Rieff's terms, the age of genocide, a period in which we have witnessed a particularly volatile reemergence of evil that is troubling precisely because we have perhaps lost not only the moral ability, but the cognitive ability to recognize it or even name it.

Social theorists such as Zygmunt Bauman and Norbert Elias have noted, each in their different ways, that modern civilization is a condition in which good and evil present themselves together. To the Enlightenment minds, there was a troubling aspect to the pairing of good and evil, for part of the "grand design" of the Enlightenment project was that, through the march of time, the former was supposed to displace the latter. Yet it is the very technologies that are supposed to eradicate evil – the media, the rise of systems of mass education, more refined and differentiated political systems – that have also contributed to the emergence of new forms of cruelty and, ironically, to the maskings of their painful truths. Hegel is wrong to assume a telos of good or evil in world history; modernity is an engine that drives good and evil and if, indeed, we live in a postmodern era, it is an era in which new engines drive the history of good and evil in different directions.

Barbarism lurks beneath the veneer of civility and not so much as a foreign body, but as an integral part of the very constitution of modernity. Its existence itself is troubling to the modern consciousness, but even more troubling is its *unpredictability*: we simply do not know when or where it will emerge. This unpredictability, as much as the existence of evil itself, is a constant source of consternation for the liberal mind. No one predicted that Sarajevo would be transformed from a metaphor of human cooperation into an abject symbol of hell on earth. Bosnia itself became a metaphor of how far we could fall so fast, of the existence of evil, geographically only hours away and in the media only nanoseconds away from the comforting "good" of capitalist, liberal democracy. The evil that supplanted the good in Bosnia was, however, near the "surface" of present time, inchoate and unseen, waiting to be put into play by specific agents in particular times and places who, through their actions, make history.

Perhaps there is a new logic of evil in postmodernity. Agency exists in a cultural context of swirling simulacra in which claims for some kind of truth about the world seem absurd or simply naive. Agency exists in relation to new forms of global media and information flows that allow agents to more easily excavate history, manipulate the present, and construct futures in new and even more creative – but not necessarily progressive – ways. This dialectic is likely to yield new expressions of evil that, at present, we can only imagine.

Notes

1 After completing this essay, I discovered that John Kekes had written a paper by the same title ("The Reflexivity of Evil," *Social Philosophy and Policy*, vol. 15, no. 1, pp. 216–32). I am grateful to Professor Kekes for allowing me to use the same title for this essay and for providing comments on my own paper, which differs rather significantly from his own in its conception of what is meant by the term "reflexivity." Also, this paper was written before the atrocities committed in Kosovo and the subsequent NATO war against Yugoslavia. As such, I have not dealt with that case at length, although the general model articulated here could be applied to interpret that case. This paper also benefited from remarks by John Rodden, Anastasia Karakasidou, and William Cain.

2 Z. Dizdarević, *Sarajevo: A War Journal*, New York, Fromm International, 1993, p. 15.

3 M. Bernstein, "Homage to the Extreme: The Shoah and the Rhetoric of Catastrophe," *The Times Literary Supplement*, March 6, 1996, p. 6.

4 N. Sanford and C. Comstock, "Sanctions for Evil," in N. Sanford, C. Comstock and Associates (eds), *Sanctions for Evil: Sources of Social Destructiveness*, San Francisco, Jossey Bass, 1973, p. 5.

5 J. Alexander, "Why Sociology Needs a Concept of Evil," unpublished manuscript.

6 N. Luhmann, *The Differentiation of Society*, New York, Columbia University Press, 1982.

7 One of the key works that recognize that the character of evil acts is to be found in the acts themselves and in subjectivity is J. Katz's *Seductions of Crime: The Moral and Sensual Attractions of Doing Evil*, New York, Basic Books, 1988. Katz establishes the basis for the sociology of evil when he notes that crime is not just a "fall from grace, but an act of 'genuine experiential creativity'" (p. 8).

8 A. Rosenthal, *A Good Look at Evil*, Philadelphia, Temple, 1987, p. 3.

9 N. Smelser, "Some Determinants of Destructive Behavior," *Sanctions for Evil*, p. 16.

10 Kekes, "The Reflexivity of Evil," p. 217.

11 W. James, *The Varieties of Religious Experience*, New York, Modern Library, 1994, p. 140.

12 Giddens conceives of modernity as "a runaway engine of enormous power which . . . threatens to push out of control and which could rend itself asunder" (*The Consequences of Modernity*, Stanford, Stanford University Press, 1991, p. 139). Given this almost Biblical rendition of modernity, which does show some axiological trace of evil, it follows that agents and agency are directed toward the restoration of the positive senses of existence.

13 Alexander also notes this elision of evil in the work of one of the foremost action

theorists, Jürgen Habermas. See J. Alexander, "Why Sociology Needs a Concept of Evil."

14 See, for instance, M. Emirbayer and A. Mirsch, "What is Agency?," *American Journal of Sociology*, vol. 103, pp. 962–1023.

15 I am positing here a formal rather than a moral sense of reflexivity, a process in which an entity thinks back upon itself and invests the products of a reflection at one point of time in another point of time as a basis for ongoing action. That actions considered excessively transgressive or cruel could not be considered to be reflexive from this point of view would be odd, as if to say that people who commit such acts do not think about them, when the evidence shows that they are oftentimes precisely thoughtful about such actions.

16 Emirbayer and Mirsch, "What is Agency?," p. 1012.

17 Emirbayer and Mirsch, "What is Agency?," p. 1012.

18 This is not to say that the interpretive model put forth in the following pages could not be applied to the actions of either the Croatian or Bosniak (Muslim) side in the war. Indeed, it would be a mistake to assume that those who are victims of evil do not, in turn, perpetrate their own evil acts (indeed, the acts of vengeance which so often take the form of atrocity are often well-planned, creative, and patiently executed).

19 V. Čubrilović, "Deportation of the Albanians," *The Roots of Serbian Aggression: Debates, Documents, Cartographic Reviews*, Bože Čović (ed.), Centar za strane jezike, Zagreb, 1993, pp. 114–41. Čubrilović was notable in Balkan history as one of the seven young radicals who were part of the plot to kill Archduke Franz Ferdinand. Sentenced to prison and later released, he went on to become a minister in Tito's government. Toward the end of his long life, he participated in the drafting of the infamous 1986 Memorandum of the Serbian Academy of Arts and Sciences, a document which many consider to be the blueprint for the Serbian war against the newly independent states of the former Yugoslavia.

20 Čubrilović, "Deportation of the Albanians," pp. 119–20.

21 The attack on religion is central to the plan: "Albanians are most sensitive in religious matters. That is where they should be hit hardest. It can be done by molesting their clergy, ploughing their graveyards, prohibiting polygamy." The most effective tool is the use of force:

> Our colonists should be given arms, if necessary. . . . A horde of Montenegrins from the mountains should be sent down to provoke massive clashes with Albanians. . . . With the help of our secret forces, the conflict should be prepared in advance. . . . The whole case should be calmly presented as a conflict between clans and tribes and, if necessary, it should be characterized in economic terms . . . some local uprisings can be provoked which would later be put down by blood . . . this should not be done directly by the army, but rather by our colonizers. . . .
>
> (pp. 121–2)

22 The document is reprinted in its entirety in B. Magas, *The Destruction of Yugoslavia: Tracking the Break-up 1980–92*, London and New York, Verso, 1993, pp. 49–52,

23 Magas, *The Destruction of Yugoslavia*, p. 51.

24 This document is reprinted in its entirety in Magas, *The Destruction of Yugoslavia*, pp. 55–61.

25 Magas, *The Destruction of Yugoslavia*, p. 57.

26 Magas, *The Destruction of Yugoslavia*, p. 57.

27 Quoted in T. Judah, *The Serbs: History, Myth, and the Destruction of Yugoslavia*, New Haven, Yale University Press, 1997, p. 164.

28 John Kekes' definition of a wicked person is one who is ruled by his or her vices and who is an habitual evildoer. The concept of "wickedness" is a serious topic in philosophy, but, strangely, in sociology has not emerged as a social type, in George Simmel's sense, even though the century seems to offer ample empirical evidence for the existence of such a type, not only in "great men" in the course of history, but in the actions of ordinary men at the level of everyday life.

29 John Kekes, "The Reflexivity of Evil," p. 218. Kekes and I differ somewhat in that he considers most evil to be the result of non-autonomous actions in which actors "do evil but they do not see what they do *as* evil" (pp. 218–19), whereas I would argue that much evil is autonomous, freely chosen, and conscious. Actors are often quite aware of what they are doing and, in some cases, as Sigmund Freud, Jack Katz, and others have pointed out, actually revel in and are energized by it.

30 The actual indictment of Ratko Mladić and Radovan Karadžić can be found in T. Cushman and S. G. Meštrović, *This Time We Knew: Western Responses to Genocide in Bosnia*, New York, New York University Press, 1996, pp. 363–84.

31 D. Binder, "Pariah as Patriot: Ratko Mladić," *New York Times Magazine*, September 4, 1994, p. 26.

32 For a detailed account, see D. Rhode, *Endgame: The Betrayal and Fall of Srebrenica, Europe's Worst Massacre since World War II*, New York, Farrar, Straus and Giroux, 1997.

33 Quoted in M. Danner, "Bosnia: The Great Betrayal," *The New York Review of Books*, vol. 45, no. 5, 1998, p. 48.

34 Quoted in M. Danner, "Bosnia," p. 40.

35 "Sixty Minutes," CBS broadcast, September 17, 1995.

36 The placement of atrocities in Bosnia as part of the long durée of European attempts to cleanse Europe of others, namely Jews *and* Muslims, can be seen in a fascinating article by Richard Rubenstein, "Holocaust and Holy War," *Annals of the American Academy of Political Social Science*, vol. 548 (November 1996), pp. 23–44.

37 This interchange between Western observers and local Balkan actors is discussed by K. Doubt, "We Had to Jump Over the Moral Bridge," *The Conceit of Innocence: Losing the Conscience of the West in the War against Bosnia*, S. Meštrović (ed.), College Station, Texas A&M University Press, 1997, pp. 120–41.

38 E. Scarry, *The Body in Pain: The Making and Unmaking of the World*, New York, Oxford University Press, 1985, p. 51.

39 Scarry, *The Body in Pain*, p. 57.

40 Scarry, *The Body in Pain*, p. 69.

41 G. W. F. Hegel, *Lectures on the Philosophy of World History: Introduction, Reason in History*, Cambridge, Cambridge University Press, 1980, pp. 42–3.

6   Others and Aliens
Between Good and Evil

Richard Kearney

I

I propose to explore here the question of alterity in terms of two main approaches. On the one hand, an *aporetics of hospitality* represented by Derridean deconstruction. On the other, an *ethics of judgement* inspired by Ricoeurian hermeneutics. While the former privileges an unconditional welcome to the undecidable other (*hostis/hospis*), the latter recommends a conditional openness to otherness based on the need for some hermeneutic discernment between good and evil.

I will try to show how these approaches respond in turn to two main categories of evil: involuntary and voluntary. Involuntary evil is traditionally associated with non-human origins – cosmological, theological, terratological. Here we might list natural calamities such as earthquakes, illness or pestilence, demon possession, and, in more recent times, alien invasion. Here humans are not considered responsible for evil, and the appropriate response is deemed to be one of lament or acquiescence. (There is literally nothing to be done but to suffer what befalls us.) The second category, "voluntary evil," attributes the origin of evil largely to humans and lays responsibility for evil happenings accordingly on human beings. Here we are dealing with anthropological evil, entailing the attribution of moral accountability.

In this essay I will focus on that liminal interface between others and aliens which, I submit, haunts our postmodern unconscious. I take the term "other" – as frequently invoked by contemporary continental theory – to refer to an alterity worthy of reverence, esteem, and welcome (hospitality). I take the term "alien," by contrast, to refer to that experience of alterity associated with selection (as in immigration policy and other acts of differentiating between natives and strangers) or sometimes with suspicion (as in UFOs). My argument here is that we need a "deconstructive-hermeneutic" capable of addressing the dialectic of others and aliens by means of a practical wisdom that enables us to take ethical decisions and actions without succumbing to the logic of sectarian exclusion. While deconstruction is needed to acknowledge the other in the alien and the alien in the other – upsetting hard-and-fast prejudices – critical hermeneutics helps us to discern between benign and malign strangers, reminding us that not every other is innocent, just as not every alien is evil. My question is basically this: How can we relate the perennial enigma of evil to the equally perennial enigma of alterity? My hypothesis is that these two enigmas overlap in the phenomenon of the "alien."

Let me begin with some observations from popular culture. It is surely not insignificant that sites concerning "aliens" are among those that receive the most frequent number of "hits" on the Internet. These include websites dealing with paranormal events as various as extraterrestrial landings, UFO sightings, alien abductions, Roswell spacecrafts, Area 21 leaks, Heavensgate, the Waco Massacre (Koresh's Branch Davidians referred to New Jerusalem as a "Space Ship"), MJ-12 conspiracies, and other cover-ups of paranormal phenomena, mainly along the Mexican border.

What's being played out on the Web is paralleled in the media generally and on TV and in cinema in particular. The hysteria and paranoia associated with alienology are best evidenced in the visual media. These serve both to screen (display) and screen off (conceal) our unconscious fears. They function as a phantasmagoria of our collective imagination, showing and hiding our deepest anxieties at one and the same time. Concerning TV, one might mention here the extraordinary success of the *X Files*, with its tantalizing leitmotif "there's something out there," and the enduringly popular *Star Trek* series. Film-wise, we could cite the recent spate of Hollywood box-office hits dealing with alien monsters and invasions – *Men in Black, Independence Day, Mars Attack, Contact, Sphere, Spawn, Alien Resurrection, The Fifth Element, Star Wars* revivals, and so on. While each of these films merits an analysis in itself, suffice it to note here that most evince a common preoccupation with alien figures who invade and assume the appearance of a human self. This usually results in the enigmatic scenario of outsider as insider. The self becomes host, often unbeknownst to itself, to some extra-terrestrial alterity. The ego undergoes an experience of abduction, possession, or invasion from without. Nowhere is this more graphically displayed than in the *Alien* series, where Lieutenant Ripley is inhabited by the monster who grows inside her until it eventually bursts through her torso. Like Freud's "uncanny," the unfamiliar returns under the guise of the familiar. The stranger surprises us through the visage of the local, homely, domestic, and normal.[1]

This enigma of the uncanny is, as Freud noted, basic to the human psyche at all times, but what I'm suggesting here is that the uncanny phenomenon of alien-invasion is at the present time dramatically foregrounded in the collective imaginary of our postmodern culture. The present time is a very specific one as we begin the second millennium with its apocalyptic overtones, and as the external enemies that served our scapegoating needs in recent decades begin to dissolve and disappear – the Soviet Bloc, South-East Asia, Cuba, Nicaragua, Iran, Libya, and Iraq. In other words, aliens proliferate where anxieties loom as to who we are and how we demarcate ourselves from others (who are not us). Alien-ation, as a postmodern phenomenon, is inseparable from the them-and-us syndrome.

Perhaps nowhere is this identity crisis more obvious than in the most Western of all Western nations, America. Here we have the phenomenon of *mondalienation* (to juggle with a phrase of Derrida's) writ large – and in large white letters on a shining hill called Hollywood. If America is indeed the unconscious of Europe, as Wim Wenders argued, then California is the unconscious of America: the last refuge of the exiled dreams and desires that made this nation what it is. There's nowhere else to go once you get to the West Coast, the westernmost extreme of the Western world, the final extremity. And Hollywood is, finally, the unconscious of that unconscious, the silver screen where the repressed returns to haunt and fascinate us.

As we begin the new millennium, more and more of us are becoming "men-in-black" invigilating each other's innocuous visages for traces of alien invasion – as in the opening sequence of the film of that name, where the FBI agents hit upon extraterrestrial aliens as they check on immigrant aliens along the Mexican border. Perhaps the fear is that we won't be able to detect the uncanny stranger until it is too late, like the unsuspecting wife – also in *Men in Black* – who welcomes her husband back after an alien abduction only to discover his face disintegrating as the alien within him makes its presence felt. But the most terrifying discovery is that the alien is not just within our family and friends but *within ourselves*. The foreigner haunts the sanctuary of the self. Our own double.

II

Before taking a closer look at the genesis of this contemporary drama of *identity*, intimately linked to the drama of *legitimation*, let me return to the philosophical discussions of evil.

One of the oldest conundrums of human thought is: *unde malum?* Where does evil come from? What are the origins of evil – human, natural, super-natural? What is the character of evil – sin, suffering, catastrophe, death? Deconstruction cautions against a rush to judgement. While not for a moment denying that evil exists, Derrida and certain other postmodern thinkers counsel vigilance. The tendency of our media society, so prone to hysteria, is to anathematize anything that is unfamiliar as "evil." The other thus becomes the alien, the stranger the scapegoat, the dissenter the devil. And it is this proclivity to demonize alterity as a threat to our collective identity that so easily issues in paranoid fantasies about invading enemies. Any threat to "national security" is met with immediate defense-attack mechanisms. One thinks of McCarthy's blacklists and Reagan's Star Wars, the Soviet show trials and gulags, Mao's cultural revolution and Tiananmen Square, the embargo of Cuba and the mining of Managua, the bombing of Cambodia and the sinking of the Rainbow Warrior, Bloody Sunday and the introduction of internment without trial in Ulster, *Kristallnacht* and Auschwitz, Satilla and Chabrilla, Sarajevo and Kosovo. The list is interminable.

Most nation-states bent on preserving their body politic from alien viruses seek to pathologize and purge their adversaries. Faced with a threatening outsider, the best mode of defense becomes attack. Again and again the national *we* is defined over and against the alien *them*. That's one reason borders exist, with nationals "in" and aliens "out." You can, of course, cross the border with the right passport and become an alien resident (like myself). But to be truly *nationalized,* you need more – not always readily available if you happen to be arriving from beneath the Rio Grande or beyond the Gaza strip. National security draws a *cordon sanitaire* around the nation-state, protecting it from alien trespassers. Like the line drawn in sand at the Alamo. Or the Mason–Dixon line. Or other lines separating north and south – in Vietnam, in Korea, in Lebanon, in Ireland.

It is in the context of such partitioning and polarizing that Derrida has pursued the question of justice and hospitality in recent years. Every nation-state is logocentric to the extent that it excludes those who do not conform (non-a) to its identity logic (a is a). This is necessary up to a point, as even the cosmopolitan Kant recognized when he accepted the need to issue conditions for refugee visitors to a state (e.g., that their sojourn be temporary, law-abiding, and non-divisive).[2] The world belongs to everyone, yes, but within the borders of nation-states, it belongs to some more than others. Granted, some form of immigration/emigration laws are inevitable. That's the law and Derrida accepts this; but he goes on to argue that there's something beyond the law: namely, justice. And justice demands more: unconditional hospitality to the alien. Hospitality is only truly just, this argument goes, when it resists the temptation to discriminate between good or evil others, that is, between the hostile enemy (*hostis*) and the benign host (hospis).

Derrida has much to say about such alienology in his book, *De l'hospitalité.*[3] As we generally understand it, the subject of hospitality is a generous host who decides, as master *chez lui,* whom to invite into his home. But it is precisely because of such sovereign self-possession that the host comes to fear certain others who threaten to invade his house, transforming him from a host into a hostage. The laws of hospitality thus reserve the right of each host to evaluate, select, and choose those he wishes to include or exclude – that is, to discriminate. Such discrimination, indispensable to the "law of hospitality" (*hospitalité en droit*), requires that each visitor identify and name him/herself before entering one's home. And this identification process involves at least some degree of violence. Derrida comments astutely on this paradox:

> There can be no sovereignty in the classic sense without the sovereignty of the self in its own home, but since there is no hospitality without

finitude, sovereignty can only operate by filtering, choosing and therefore excluding and doing violence. A certain injustice . . . is present
from the outset, at the very threshold of the right to hospitality. This
collusion between the violence of power or the force of law (*Gewalt*) on
the one hand, and hospitality on the other, seems to be radically integral
to the very inscription of hospitality as a right.[4]

Derrida goes on to link this inclusive/exclusive law of hospitality with ethics
in the more general sense. The paradox of the stranger (*xenos/hostis*) as
either invader-alien or welcome-other "extends from the circumscribed field
of *ethos* or ethics, of habitation or visitation as *ethos*, of *Sittlichkeit*, of
objective morality as specifically identified in Hegel's threefold determination
of right and the philosophy of right: *family, society* (civil or bourgeois) and
state (or nation-state)."[5] Derrida sums up the aporia of the alien-other thus:
"the outsider (*hostis*) received as host or as enemy. Hospitality, hostility,
hostipitality."[6] Fully cognizant of the way this undecidable dialectic con-
founds our ethical conventions, Derrida affirms the priority of a hospitality
of justice – open to the absolute other as another without name. Here we
supersede the hospitality of law. What distinguishes the absolute other is that
he is without distinction, that is, without name or proper name. And the
absolute or unconditional hospitality that he deserves marks a break with
everyday conventions of hospitality governed by rights, contracts, duties,
and pacts. Absolute hospitality, argues Derrida,

> requires that I open my home and that I give not only to the stranger
> (furnished with a family name and the social status of a stranger, etc.)
> but to the absolute other, unknown and anonymous; and that I give
> place (*donne lieu*), let come, arrive, let him take his place in the place that
> I offer him, without demanding that he give his name or enter into some
> reciprocal pact.[7]

If absolute hospitality requires us to break with the accredited hospitality of
right, this doesn't mean repudiating the latter out of hand; it may even
mean, concedes Derrida, preserving it in a state of perpetual progress and
mutation. What it does mean, however, is that absolute hospitality is as
heterogeneous to conditional hospitality as justice is to the law of right with
which it is tied.[8]

But Derrida adds a telling coda to this dazzling deconstruction of the
"right of hospitality." The other is not just the alien stranger, utterly external
to home, family, nation, or state. That would be to relegate the other to
absolute exteriority – barbarous, savage, precultural, and prejuridical. No, in
order that hospitality be just, we must allow some way for the absolute other
to enter our home, family, nation, state. And that is why justice can never
dispense with the law of right: "The relation to the alien/stranger (*l'étranger*)
is regulated by the law of right (*le droit*), by the becoming-right of justice."[9]

The difficulty with this analysis of hospitality is that it seems to preclude our need to differentiate between good and evil aliens, between benign and malign strangers, between saints and psychopaths (though admittedly 99 per cent of us fall somewhere between the two). If hospitality is to remain absolutely just and true, all incoming others must remain unidentifiable and undecidable. Derrida appears to claim as much when he declares that

> for pure hospitality or pure gift to occur there must be absolute surprise . . . an opening without horizon of expectation . . . to the newcomer whoever that may be. The newcomer may be good or evil, but if you exclude the possibility that the newcomer is coming to destroy your house, if you want to control this and exclude this terrible possibility in advance, there is no hospitality. . . . The other, like the Messiah, must arrive whenever he or she wants.[10]

For Derrida, aliens only come in the dark (like thieves in the night), and we are always in the dark when they come. We are never sure who or what they are; we cannot even be sure if we are hallucinating or not. For the absolute other is without name and without face, an "impossible, unimaginable, unforseeable, unbelievable, absolute surprise."[11] The best we can do is try to read between the lines and make a leap of faith, an impossible leap of faith, like Abraham, like Kierkegaard. But why not add – and here's my difficulty with the undecidable – "like Jim Jones or David Koresh" or other figures of mystical madness who believe they are recipients of messianic messages from some Other they call God?

If all reading is reading in the dark, how can we discern between holy and unholy spirits, how distinguish between the deities of peace and justice and those of horror and destruction? Joseph Campbell, for one, has much to say about messianic monsters in *The Power of Myth*, a cautionary reminder (it seems to me) of the need for some kind of ethical decision: "By monster I mean some horrendous presence or apparition that explodes all your standards for harmony, order and ethical conduct. . . . That's God in the role of destroyer. Such experiences go past ethical judgements. Ethics is wiped out . . . God is horrific."[12]

To be absolutely hospitable is to suspend all criteria of ethical or juridical discrimination. And in such non-discriminate openness to alterity we find ourselves unable to differentiate between good and evil, which is a fine lesson in tolerance but not necessarily in moral judgement. If there *is* a difference between Jesus and Jim Jones, between Saint Francis and Stalin, between Melena and Mengele, between Siddhartha and the Marquis de Sade – and I think most of us would want to say there is – then some further philosophical reflections are needed to supplement the deconstructive gesture of hospitality. Deconstructive non-judgementalism needs to be supplemented, I suggest, with a hermeneutics of practical wisdom.

III

Deconstruction is not the only postmodern response to the challenge of evil. While I grant that it is a necessary condition of postmodern wisdom, I do not believe it is a sufficient one. There is also the need for a critical hermeneutics of action. For if deconstruction makes us more intellectually sensitive to the complex and often interchangeable nature of others and aliens, alerting us to the irreducible alterity of all incomers, hermeneutics addresses the need for critically informed ethico-political judgement. It's not enough to be open to the other (though this is essential to ethics); one must also be careful to discern, in some provisional fashion at least, between good and evil.

In an essay entitled, "Evil, A Challenge to Philosophy and Theology," Paul Ricoeur offers a hermeneutic critique of different discursive responses to evil: lament and blame, myth, wisdom, and theodicy.[13]

The first discursive response – *lament* and *blame* (witnessed in the Hebrew Bible, for example) – differentiates between evil as suffering and evil as wrongdoing. Lament refers to an evil that befalls us from outside. By contrast, blame refers to evil that arises from within us and for which we are responsible. Or to put it another way, if lament sees us as victims, blame makes culprits of us.[14] The fact is, of course, that these two categories are almost always intertwined. We can feel guilty for committing an evil act while simultaneously experiencing seduction, or invasion, by an overwhelming force outside of us. But for the moment, we'll let the distinction stand.

The next discursive genre – *myth* – allows for the incorporation of evil into "great narratives of origin" (Mircea Eliade). These genealogical narratives seek to explain the origin of evil in terms of the genesis of the cosmos (cosmogony). They offer a "plot" which configures the monstrosity of evil, explaining the source of the obscene and thereby taking some of the shock out of it. Such mythic spectacles make the foreign curiously familiar, the unbearable bearable, the outrageous accessible.[15] In mythological legends, considerations of human moral choice are inextricably linked to cosmological cycles of fate, destiny, or predestination. The evil figure is the alienated figure, that is, a self determined by some force beyond itself.

Myth proceeds towards *wisdom* – our next discursive category – to the extent that we not only recount the origins of evil but also seek to justify why such is the case for each one of us. In short, while myth narrates, wisdom argues.[16] It seeks to address the question not only of *why* but *why me?* The wisdom genre turns lament into a legal complaint. It tries to make moral sense of the monstrous. An exemplary case here is the Book of Job, where God and man engage in dialogue about the nature of creation and covenant. With such wisdom literature, the enigma of evil becomes less a matter of metaphysical givenness than of interpersonal relations (human–human or human–divine). In the conclusion to Job, arguments about retribution and justice are ultimately turned to a contemplative wisdom of love: Job learns to love Yahweh "for naught" in defiance of Satan's wager at the outset of the story.

Wisdom discourse gives way to "speculative" discourse with the development of Christian theology. Augustine is the first great advocate of this position in his answer to the gnostics. In order to show that evil is not a substance implanted in the universe but a punishment (*poena*) for human sin (*peccatum*), Augustine invents a new category, "nothingness" (*nihil*). Evil is now construed as a deficiency in being which amounts to a privation of goodness (*privatio boni*). If there is evil in the world, therefore, it can only be the result of human action – that is, an act of turning away from the good being of God towards a lack of being. Augustine thus proposes a radically moral vision of evil which replaces the genealogical question, *Unde malum?*, with the question of willful human wrongdoing, *Unde malum faciamus?* The cause of evil is not to be found in cosmology but in some form of willed action – the sins of the "bad will." This leads in turn, of course, to a penal view of history where no one suffers unjustly. Everyone gets his or her reward, and all pain is a recompense for sin.

The difficulty for Augustine and subsequent theology was how to reconcile this extreme hypothesis of moral evil with the need to give sin a "supraindividual" and historical-generic account in order to explain how suffering is not always justly apportioned as a retribution for individual sins. In countless cases it is clearly excessive. In other words, if evil is something we as humans do, it is also *done to us*: something we inherit, something already there. Augustine thus sought to reinterpret the *Genesis* tale of original sin in order to rationalize this apparently irrational paradox: namely, we are responsible but not *entirely* responsible for the evil we commit or endure.

It was but a short step from these Augustinian speculations on original sin to the fully-fledged theories of Western onto-theology. Thus we find Leibniz, for example, invoking the principle of Sufficient Reason to account for the judicious balancing of good with evil in the "best of all possible worlds." And if this balancing act of retribution and compensation is attributed to the infinite mind of God by Leibniz, it is dialectically humanized by Hegel and the German Idealists. Hegel's "cunning of reason" silences the scandal of suffering by subsuming the tragic into a triumphant logic where all that is real is rational. Here the hubris of systematic speculation reaches its untenable extreme: "The more the system flourishes, the more its victims are marginalized. The success of the system is its failure. Suffering, as what is expressed by the voices of lamentation, is what the system excludes."[17]

But neither version of theodicy – Leibnizian or Hegelian – can provide a convincing answer to the protest of unjust suffering: *Why me?* This protest rightly and righteously continues to echo through the memoirs of evil from Job and Gethsemane to Hiroshima and Auschwitz. Nor can theodicy resist the debunking of "rational theology" in part three of Kant's *Critique of Pure*

Reason. Indeed the greatness of Kant was to recognize the need to pass from a purely "theoretical" explanation of evil to a more "practical" one. This move from speculative explanation to moral-political action liberates the insight that evil is something that ought not to be and needs to be struggled against. By de-alienating evil and making it a matter of contingency rather than necessity (cosmogonic, theological, metaphysical, or historical), Kant brought us face to face with the responsibility of action.

I might add here that if Kant freed us from the excess of rationalist speculation on evil, he also warned against the opposite extreme of drunken irrationalism (what he called *Schwärmerei*), the sort of mystical madness which submits to evil as an alien power that invades and overwhelms us at a whim. This latter view typifies not only belief in demonic possession but also the mystical profession of the "dark side of God" running from the gnostics and Bruno to Boehme, Schelling, and Jung (e.g., *Answer to Job*). By taking the mystique out of evil, Kant removed some of its captivating power. He enabled us to see that evil is not a property of some external demon or deity but a phenomenon deeply bound up with the anthropological condition. Evil ceases to be a matter of paranoid projection and sacrificial scapegoating and becomes instead an affair of human responsibility. Absolutist dualities are overcome. One's self becomes oneself-as-another and one's other becomes another-as-oneself.

But even Kant could not totally ignore the aporetic character of evil. For if he clearly called for a response within the limits of practical human reason, he could never completely deny some residual inscrutability (*Unerforschbarkeit*) of evil. At one point, Kant states that there may be "no conceivable ground from which the moral evil in us could originally have come."[18] The lament of *Why? Why me? Why my beloved child?* remains as troublingly enigmatic as ever. Victims of evil cannot be silenced with either rational explanation (theodicy) or irrational submission (mysticism). Their stories cry out for other responses capable of addressing both the alterity and the humanity of evil.

But do such responses exist? How may we acknowledge the enigma of evil, laid bare by our detour through Western genres of thought, while addressing Tolstoy's question: *What is to be done*? Taking a further cue from Ricoeur's hermeneutic reading, I will propose a two-fold approach: practical understanding (*phronesis–mimesis–praxis*) and working-through (*catharsis–Durcharbeitung*).

"Practical understanding" is the name I give to that limited capacity of the human mind to *think* the enigma of evil. I draw here from such varied models as biblical "wisdom" (discussed above), Aristotle's "practical wisdom" (*phronesis*), Kant's "practical reason" (indeterminate judgement), and Ricoeur's "narrative understanding." What each of these models has in common is an ability to transfer the aporia of evil from the sphere of theory (*theoria*) – proper to the exact knowledge criteria of logic, science, and speculative metaphysics – to the sphere of a more practical art of understanding (*techne/praxis*), which allows for an approximative grasp of phenomena: what Aristotle calls "the flexible rule of the architect." Where speculative theory, epitomized by theodicy, explained evil in terms of ultimate causal or creationist origins, practical understanding is geared towards a more hermeneutic comprehension of the indeterminate, contingent, and singular characteristics of evil – while not abandoning all claim to quasi-universal criteria (that would account for at least a minimally shared sense of evil). Such practical understanding borrows from action the conviction that evil is something that ought not to be and must be struggled against. In that sense, it resists the fatalism of archeologies of evil – mythical and theodical – in favor of a future-oriented praxis. The response (though by no means the solution) offered by practical understanding is to act against evil. Instead of acquiescing in the face of an origin that precedes us, action turns our understanding towards the future "by the idea of a *task* to be accomplished." The moral-political requirement to act does not therefore abandon the legitimate quest for some minimal model of reasonable discernment; it in fact demands it. For how could we act against evil if we could not identify it, that is, if we could not critically discern between good and evil? In this respect, the genuine struggle against evil presupposes a critical hermeneutic of suspicion. And such hermeneutic understanding retains Kant's insistence on a practical reason that seeks to think somehow the unthinkable. And to do so with the "sobriety of a thinking always careful not to transgress the limits of knowledge."[19]

Our critical understanding of evil may never surpass the provisional nature of Kant's indeterminate (that is, "aesthetic reflective") judgement. But it at least judges, and in a manner alert to both the singular alterity of evil and to its quasi-universal character as grasped by the *sensis communis*. Not exact or adequate judgement but a form of judgement for all that, based on the practical wisdom conveyed by narratives and driven by moral justice. We may say, accordingly, that practical judgement is not only "phronetic" but "narrative" in character. An overlapping of *phronesis* (Aristotle) and judgement (Kant) neatly captured in Ricoeur's account of the ethical role of narrative:

> Ethics as Aristotle conceived it, and as it can still be conceived today, speaks abstractly of the relation between virtue and the pursuit of happiness. It is the function of poetry in its narrative and dramatic form, to propose to the imagination and to its mediation various figures that constitute so many *thought experiments* by which we learn to link together the ethical aspects of human conduct and happiness and misfortune. By means of poetry we learn how reversals of fortune result from this or that conduct, as this is constructed by the plot in the narrative. It is due to the familiarity we have with the types of plot received from our culture that we learn to relate virtues, or rather forms of excellence, with happiness or unhappiness. These "lessons" of poetry

constitute the "universals" of which Aristotle spoke; but these are universals that are of a lower degree than those of logic and theoretical thought. We must none the less speak of understanding but in the sense that Aristotle gave to *phronesis*. . . . In this sense I am prepared to speak of phronetic understanding in order to contrast it with theoretical understanding. Narrative belongs to the former and not to the latter.[20]

If practical understanding addresses the action-response to evil, it sometimes neglects the suffering-response. Evil is not just something we struggle against, it is also (as noted above) something we undergo. To ignore this passivity of evil suffered is to ignore the extent to which evil strikes us as shockingly strange and disempowering. It is also to underestimate that irreducible alterity of evil which myth and theodicy tend to overestimate. One of the wisest responses to evil is, on this count, to acknowledge its traumatizing effects and work-them-through (*durcharbeiten*) as best we can. Practical understanding can only redirect us toward action if it has already recognized that an element of alterity almost always attaches to evil, especially when it concerns illness, horror, catastrophe, or death. No matter how prepared we are to make sense of evil, we are never prepared enough. That is why the "work of mourning" is so important as a way of not allowing the inhuman nature of suffering to result in a complete "loss of self" (what Freud called "melancholia"). Some kind of catharsis is necessary to prevent the slide into fatalism that all too often issues in despairing self-destruction. The critical detachment brought about by cathartic mourning elicits a wisdom that turns *passive lament* into the possibility of *active complaint, that is, protest*.[21]

The role played by narrative testimonies is crucial in this respect, whether it be those of survivors of the Holocaust or of trauma-abuse. For such narrative rememberings invite the victim to escape the alienation of evil, that is, to move from a position of mute helplessness to speech-acts of revolt and (where possible) self-renewal. Some kind of narrative working-through is necessary, it seems, for survivors of evil not to feel crippled by grief or guilt (about the death of others and their own survival) nor to succumb to the game of the "expiatory victim." What the catharsis of mourning-narrative allows is that new actions are still possible *in spite of evil suffered.* It detaches us from the obsessional repetitions and repressions of the past and frees us for a future. For only thus can we escape the disabling cycles of retribution, fate, and destiny: cycles which *estrange* us from our power to act by instilling the view that evil is overpoweringly alien – that is, irresistible. Working-through the experience of evil – narratively, practically, cathartically – enables us to take the allure out of evil so that we can begin to distinguish between possible and impossible modes of protest and resistance. Working-through is central to a hermeneutics of action. It makes evil resistible.

In sum, by transforming the alienation and victimization of lament into a moral response of just struggle, the hermeneutics of action offers, I submit, an answer (if not a solution) to the challenge of evil.

IV

Let me return, finally, to the question of aliens in our postmodern culture. The postmodern paranoia around aliens is not adventitious. It is, I believe, a symptom informing the current anxiety about identity-questions – Who are we? What is our nation? Why us? This crisis of *identity* is inseparable (as noted) from a crisis of *legitimation*. This is, of course, a world-wide phenomenon, but it is especially acute, I believe, in the Western world, and nowhere more so than in the "cultural unconscious" of the Western world – America.[22]

If philosophy is to address this postmodern drama of identity and legitimation, I would suggest it might begin by, first, deconstructing all hard and fast polarizations between others and aliens (and, by extension, others and selves); and, second, conducting hermeneutic analyses of the principal discourses used to represent the alterity of evil and advancing new modes of recognition and renewal. For if it is true that we need an aporetics of alterity, we also need an ethics of judgement. It is not enough to interpret our strange world, we must also take action to change it.

Notes

1 S. Freud, "The Uncanny," *The Standard Edition of the Complete Psychological Works of Sigmund Freud*, vol. 17, London, Hogarth Press, 1955.
2 See I. Kant, *Perpetual Peace and Other Essays*, trans. T. Humphrey, Cambridge, Hackett, 1983.
3 J. Derrida, *De L'hospitalité*, Paris, Calmann-Lévy, 1997. All translations from the French are my own.
4 Derrida, *De L'hospitalité*, p. 53.
5 Derrida, *De L'hospitalité*, p. 44.
6 Derrida, *De L'hospitalité*, p. 45.
7 Derrida, *De L'hospitalité*, p. 29.
8 Derrida, *De L'hospitalité*, p. 29.
9 Derrida, *De L'hospitalité*, p. 69.
10 UCD Round Table, 1997, *Questioning Ethics*, R. Kearney and M. Dooley (eds), London, Routledge, 1998.
11 J. Caputo, *The Prayers and Tears of Jacques Derrida*, Bloomington, Indiana University Press, 1997, p. 73; see also M. Dooley, "The Politics of Exodus: Derrida, Kierkegaard and Levinas on 'Hospitality,'" *International Kierkegaard Commentary: Works of Love*, R. Perkins (ed.), Macon, Mercer University Press, 1999.
12 J. Campbell, *The Power of Myth*, New York, Doubleday, 1988, p. 222.
13 P. Ricoeur, *Figuring the Sacred: Religion, Narrative and Imagination*, Indianapolis, Fortress Press, 1995.
14 Ricoeur, *Figuring the Sacred*, p. 250.
15 As Aristotle noted in *Poetics*, Dent, London, 1963, III, 4–iv, 3: "There is the enjoyment people always get from representations . . . we enjoy looking at accurate likenesses of things which are themselves painful to see, such as obscene beasts and corpses."
16 Ricoeur, *Figuring the Sacred*, p. 252; see also P. Ricoeur, *The Symbolism of Evil*, Boston, Beacon Press, 1967.

17 Ricoeur, *Figuring the Sacred*, p. 257.
18 I. Kant, *Religion within the Limits of Reason Alone*, New York, Harper Torchbooks, 1960, p. 38. Cited by Ricoeur, *Figuring the Sacred*, pp. 258–9.
19 Ricoeur, *Figuring the Sacred*, p. 259.
20 P. Ricoeur, "Life in Quest of Narrative," *On Paul Ricoeur: Narrative and Interpretation,* David Wood (ed.), London, Routledge, 1991, p. 23.
21 See S. Freud, "Remembering, Repeating, and Working-Through," in *The Standard Edition of the Complete Psychological Works of Sigmund Freud*, vol. 12.
22 I discuss this dialectic of "otherness" in the constitution of British, Irish, and European identities in my *Postnationalist Ireland*, London, Routledge, 1997. See also the theological relation between sacrificial scapegoating, legitimation narratives, and national identity analyzed by Regina Schwartz, *The Curse of Cain: The Violent Legacy of Monotheism*, Chicago, Chicago University Press, 1997.

Index